THE
ROMANCE
DIET

Sunstone books may be purchased for educational, business, or sales promotional use.
For information please write: Special Markets Department, Sunstone Press,
P.O. Box 2321, Santa Fe, New Mexico 87504-2321.
Cover design › Ida Jansson
Book design › Vicki Ahl
Body typeface › Garamond
Printed on acid-free paper
∞
eBook 978-1-61139-430-6

Library of Congress Cataloging-in-Publication Data

Names: Allison, Destiny, 1968-
Title: The romance diet : body image and the wars we wage with ourselves / by
Destiny Allison.
Description: Santa Fe : Sunstone Press, 2015. | Includes bibliographical
references and index.
Identifiers: LCCN 2015032150 | ISBN 9781632930903 (softcover : alk. paper)
Subjects: LCSH: Allison, Destiny, 1968- | Overweight persons--Biography. |
Obesity--Popular works. | Women sculptors--United States--Biography. |
Husband and wife.
Classification: LCC RC628 .A46 2015 | DDC 362.1963/980092--dc23
LC record available at http://lccn.loc.gov/2015032150

Sunstone Press is committed to minimizing our environmental impact on the planet. The paper used in this book is from
responsibly managed forests. Our printer has received Chain of Custody (CoC) certification from: The Forest Stewardship Council™
(FSC®), Programme for the Endorsement of Forest Certification™ (PEFC™), and The Sustainable Forestry Initiative® (SFI®).

The FSC® Council is a non-profit organization, promoting the environmentally appropriate, socially beneficial and economically
viable management of the world's forests. FSC® certification is recognized internationally as a rigorous environmental and social standard
for responsible forest management.

WWW.SUNSTONEPRESS.COM
SUNSTONE PRESS / POST OFFICE BOX 2321 / SANTA FE, NM 87504-2321 /USA
(505) 988-4418 / ORDERS ONLY (800) 243-5644 / FAX (505) 988-1025

THE ROMANCE DIET

DIET

BODY IMAGE AND THE WARS
WE WAGE ON OURSELVES

DESTINY ALLISON

SUNSTONE
PRESS

SANTA FE

Other Books by Destiny Allison

Non-fiction:
  Shaping Destiny

Fiction:
Pipe Dreams
Bitter Root

*To the Solace Crisis Treatment Center,
women everywhere,
and my amazing Steve.*

Preface

In August of 2013, I confronted a crisis. The work I did had stripped all the cartilage from two vertebras in my back, forcing me to give up my career. I had suspected the injury was severe, but only faced it when denial threatened my marriage. A visit to the doctor confirmed my suspicions and revealed a more significant threat.

To address it, my husband and I shed a combined 120 pounds over the course of a year. I became a poster child for good cholesterol and we reinvented ourselves. The process strengthened our marriage and put age-old demons to bed, but it was a slow, long road fraught with joys and perils neither of us would have guessed.

Initially, I was terrified to tell our story. How could I reveal to the world my personal hell, my deepest shame? Eventually, I felt I didn't have a choice. We need to talk about the small things that eat at us, speak honestly about our feelings and experiences, and learn to abandon the cultural conventions that imprison our souls.

My story is not uncommon. In sharing it, I hope readers are inspired. It is my great wish that it will help women and the men who love them find peace with themselves.

1

If what I'd lost had only been a career, it would have been okay. But how do you give up everything that defines you, everything you are? I had been a steel sculptor, wresting success through muscle and sheer force of will. My art garnered respect and admiration. It made me somebody, made me strong. Then, one day while loading small sculptures into the back of our Prius, my world came suddenly to an end. The pain in my back began as a sharp twinge and grew like an August mushroom. Four hours later, I couldn't walk upright. Four more and moving at all made me scream.

Unlike previous flare ups, this one didn't end. At night, I cried out in my sleep. Hunched over and moaning, I hobbled through pain-fogged days. Whiskey became a cherished companion as I tried to blot out the pain. For a year I limped along giving the galleries minimum inventory and avoiding commissions when I could. The air in my studio grew stale from lack of use. Long sheets of steel rusted in their storage racks. My financial reserves dwindled.

When my husband Steve left for work, I stayed home and tried to write. If I could switch from one medium to another—weld words to build mass and shape and volume on paper—I could recreate myself from the ashes of what I had been. I pushed myself hard and grew. It sounds spiritual and might even have been, but the outward manifestation was simpler. I got fat.

I couldn't understand it. I ate the same as I always did. We exercised sometimes and took long hikes when we could. It didn't matter. In two years, I gained forty-four pounds. My 5'6" 140 pound frame slowly changed from lithe and athletic to sluggish and plump. The abomination of my flesh repulsed me, but didn't make sense.

One day, Steve forgot to kiss me goodbye. I came out of the bathroom to find him gone. This forced me to confront how heavy his burden had become. Though sculpting had been my primary focus, I co-owned a shopping center with him. The pain in my back and the depression it caused had forced me to abandon my responsibilities, leaving Steve to manage the enormous project alone. Now, he looked gray all the time. At night when I asked about his day, he said, "Fine." But it wasn't fine. His bright blue eyes no longer laughed. His smile, though genuine, seemed weary. He often fell asleep on the couch or in the low lamplight of my office while listening to whatever I had written that day. We seldom made love. When we did it was a surface thing, the sliding of bodies urgent and quickly over. Oh, the love was there. Just not the energy.

On quiet mornings alone in the house and struggling to learn a new craft, I told myself it wasn't my fault. In the evenings over dinner, *he* told me it wasn't my fault.

"Life happens," he said, then reached for my hand, played with my wedding band, and murmured his love. Duty done, he turned his attention to whatever happened to be on the plate in front of him—a large steak slathered with mayonnaise, another chicken thigh dripping fat.

He always asked what I wanted for dinner.

I always said the same thing. "I don't care." And I didn't.

After our children had grown and gone, I seldom cooked. I'd done enough of it to last a lifetime. When my back went out, I quit completely. Steve would stop at the store on his way home, grab what he liked, and cook for me. He enjoyed it and I had other things on my mind.

The morning he forgot to kiss me, I decided to quit hiding and get the pain in my back diagnosed. A week later, sitting in my doctor's office while he authorized the MRI scan that would confirm what I already knew, I demanded a thyroid test. My weight gain had to stem from something, right?

My doctor didn't think the test necessary. I pleaded, cajoled, and finally insisted. I desperately wanted a pill, an excuse, a way to be me again. Finally, he acquiesced and did a full blood panel. When next I met with him, he informed me that my thyroid was fine, but my cholesterol count was 436; more than twice what is considered dangerous and stroke was an imminent threat.

That night, dejected because no pill could magically change my life, I told Steve about the results. Yes, my back is shot and I'll never sculpt again. No, I don't have a thyroid problem. Oh, and by the way, my cholesterol is out of control.

He paled when I told him the number and, as always, reached for my hand. "I'm sorry about sculpting. I really am. But, honey, this cholesterol thing is important. I need you to last."

"Uh huh."

"No. Really. I need you for decades and decades." He patted his belly; that big, pregnant round preceding him wherever he went like a flag bearer precedes a king. "If yours is that bad, mine must be too," he said. "I'll do it with you. We'll do it together."

Do what? I thought. Give me back my life? My identity? But I nodded and offered a weak smile because Steve's weight bothered me more than my own. I regularly pictured the arrival of an ambulance, then paramedics hooking up the wires that would try, without success, to start his beautiful heart again.

At six feet, 245 pounds, Steve was like a big teddy bear. Though I loved it when he wrapped his arms around me, he crushed me when he laid that weight across my body. Sometimes, I felt suffocated and wished he would hurry so I could breathe. Then, of course, guilt consumed me when he asked what was wrong. How could I tell him? Criticizing or nagging him about his weight seemed not only inappropriate, but ugly. I wouldn't be that wife.

I loved this man, belly and all, and he loved me. Should I choose to dye my thin, honey-colored hair purple, cut its average length to something short and spiky, hide my brown eyes with gothic make-up, and gauge my ears, he would support me completely. If he wanted to eat an entire quart of ice cream while watching a movie, he had that right. I didn't look askance when he bought an empty shopping center at the height of the financial crisis. He didn't raise an eyebrow when I told him of my plan to stay home and write.

We worked side by side building that center into something amazing. He read, critiqued, and helped edit my books at night. How could I tell him what or how to eat?

I adored him for suggesting we lose weight together, but couldn't fathom the possibility. Neither of us believed in dieting. He loved food. I hated gyms. Besides, where would we find the time?

Daunted, I let the subject lapse and finished my stew.

2

I t turns out there are 209 calories in a cup of beef stew (depending on the ingredients), but I didn't know that then. That night, I ate two bowls and two slices of bread. Steve had three. When finished, we took our wine to the couch and streamed a movie. He fell asleep halfway through. I watched until it ended, nudged him awake, and we trundled off to bed.

I woke to the smell of frying bacon. Steve stood at the kitchen counter dicing potatoes. As I sipped my tea, he fried my eggs and served them to me with a mound of buttery home fries and three slices of bacon.

I've never been a big breakfast person, but it was Steve's favorite meal. He woke hours before me and loved to have it cooking when I staggered into the kitchen, eyes squinting against the onslaught of daylight. This morning, the sight of all that food repulsed me. I wasn't hungry yet, but not wanting to disappoint him, I broke the yolks and choked down a bite. The smell turned my stomach. Overnight, food had become the enemy.

"Maybe we could try splitting meals," I said. "Not dieting or anything, just portion control."

Looking up from the stove, his lopsided smile spoke courage I didn't have. "Couldn't hurt," he replied.

After serving himself, he joined me at the table—a thick slab of teak long enough to seat eight, bring our many children together, or spread the mail over and leave it for weeks. He shoved the mail aside to make room for his plate.

"I was thinking about it and I can't remember the last time I had a physical. I bet my cholesterol is worse than yours. Honey, let's get healthy. Let's make it happen," he said.

I nodded and pushed my food away.

"Done already?" he asked.

"It's good. Sorry, just not very hungry this morning."

Hand mid-air, omelet quivering on the tines, he fixed those warm blue eyes on me. "Everything okay?"

I looked at my hands. Gnarled with scars and swollen with weight, they mapped my life. "I wanted it to be thyroid," I said.

He set the fork down and reached for me. "I'm glad it's not."

"Why?" I asked, though I knew what he would say. Steve didn't trust meds. He had known too many people who had lost themselves in a seemingly never-ending cocktail of symptom-averting drugs, which altered personalities and destroyed lives.

"I don't want to lose you. I don't want you to change. You have no idea what those pills would do to you and neither do I," he said.

I took a breath. "So, split meals?"

He nodded, chewing.

I gestured to his plate. "This stuff is loaded with cholesterol, you know."

He arched an eyebrow and grinned. "Everything in moderation, right?"

I grabbed his hand and brought it to my lips. "Do you know how much I love you?"

"Why, yes. Yes, I do," he answered. Then his eyes grew serious. "That's why we both need to last."

We began at lunch. He closed his business for an hour and I met him at a local restaurant. There were few people in the cavernous dining room. Salvadorian needlepoint paintings and carved wood pineapples graced long walls in Latin colors—mango, pomegranate, and lime. A screen behind the bar flickered with silenced Mexican novellas. We took our favorite booth and ordered a dish we both enjoyed. Sunlight made a rectangle on the table that folded up and over Steve's bright green, too small t-shirt.

He had jumped from an extra large to a double X, but refused to buy clothes in that size. Instead, he wore what he had and let his belly show. I had never understood that about him. Some mornings he didn't even glance in the mirror. At first, I had believed his nonchalance a mask. An entrepreneur, and the smartest businessman I've ever met, he had been wildly successful when we started dating. I thought he dressed down so as not to intimidate his customers or business associates, but Steve truly didn't care what people thought—then or now—and, not surprisingly, they loved him for it. The man was chaos incarnate, but what a beautiful chaos it was; part mad scientist, part goofy kid, a ton of heart, and a cool, calm center.

For me, it was different. Though tough as nails on the outside, inside I quivered like the egg on his fork that morning. The artist in me waited always for the next rejection while the woman in me understood her role all too well. Make your man happy. Keep a clean house. Be graceful, demur, and charming. I failed at most of these things, often grotesquely, and my lack reinforced a constant self-doubt. I wanted what Steve had.

When our meal arrived, he divided it neatly in half and carefully—oh, so carefully—arranged my portion on an extra plate. The stuffed Poblano chili and black beans smelled of far away places, of a rich culture simmering in exotic heat. Cumin and garlic blended with cilantro, fresh feta, and grilled vegetables under a cream sauce thick and sweet. We took small bites, chewed them slowly to make them last, and focused on our conversation to distract ourselves from the missing volume of food.

As we talked over that first shared plate, I tried to remember the last time we had discussed so much. Usually, our interactions were sound bites between phone calls and interruptions. Broken sentences punctuated the shared rolling of our eyes as yet something else took priority over our personal lives. At home, we talked over our days and planned our next business moves, sharing the small stories of success that fueled our mutual drive. Seldom, however, did we make time for more intimate exchanges. That first lunch opened a door and we found we hungered for each other's company more than we hungered for the food. At the end of the meal, we were satisfied.

3

S oon after we began sharing our meals, I realized if I didn't also do something about Steve's stress and my depression, the efforts we made on behalf of our health would fail. I couldn't keep hiding in the fictitious worlds I created. Though I loved the work, it didn't pay.

One late afternoon in early August, I called Steve at work. "What time are you coming home?" I asked.

"Not sure. What's up?"

"I need to talk to you about something."

Through the phone, I heard Steve suck in his breath. "Everything okay?"

"Yeah. I just need to talk to you. Do you have to stay late?"

"No. I'll even try to leave a little early."

"You don't have to do that," I said.

"No. It's fine. I'll see you soon."

I set the phone down and stared out the window. Weeds intertwined with lavender stems in my neglected garden. A stinkbug meandered across a flagstone step. Like the aspen leaves on our sole surviving tree, I felt limp and colorless.

Identity is a difficult thing. Mine had been deeply tied to financial independence, physical strength, and accolades. My work had been internationally collected. Destiny Allison steel sculptures graced mansions, boulevards, luxury hotels, and law offices from New Mexico to Hong Kong. Simultaneously, I had an acute marketing mind and sharp business acumen.

I had been named Business Woman of the Year in 2011. Now, without an income and unable to trust my body, my insecurities reared. Was I still sexy? Did Steve resent my lack of a paycheck? Did he see me the way I saw myself—fat, weak, and useless? I put myself down in every conceivable way and that had to stop.

Earlier that day, I'd taken the first step by making an appointment with an audiologist. A virus in my twenties had damaged my hearing, but because I worked in solitude it hadn't really mattered. When necessary, I read lips. Most of the time, I bluffed and doing so kept the world at a safe distance. The thought of hearing again terrified me, but if I were to come out of hiding and rebuild my life, I had to risk it.

Later, I drafted the rough outline of a business plan. Now it lay sprawled across the dining room table, along with wadded up pieces of paper, gum wrappers, and a half-full glass of water. I surveyed the plan dispassionately. With a little bit of capital, the store I envisioned had a good chance of success. I just had to get Steve to agree to it.

He arrived home in record time. The car door shut with a slam and our front door flew open. "Destiny?" he bellowed.

I came around the corner and almost crashed into him. "Hey. How was your day?"

"Fine. What's up?" he said.

His whole body seemed to quiver, though he stood perfectly still. I rose on tiptoes to kiss him, then led him into the big, open room that served as kitchen, dining, and living rooms. Above the table, a spider web dangled from the pitched, wood paneled ceiling. Seeing it, I winced. The house was a mess again.

"Here," I said, thrusting a sheaf of paper at him. "Read this."

"What is it? What do you need to talk about?"

"Steve, I want to open a business."

His body relaxed. "I knew it! At first, I thought we were in trouble or that I'd done something majorly wrong, but then I—"

"No. We're fine. It's just that I need to do *something*."

"What about your books? Your writing?"

I sighed and slumped in my chair. "I love it, but it's going to take years to build the platform I need to make any money. We don't have that time right now."

His nod chastened me. My choices had worn on him.

"The book's almost done. It won't take but a day or so to finish the final draft. After that, I'm going to put the writing on hold. And I really think I've got a business idea that'll work."

"Okay. Let's hear it. What's your plan?"

"I want to open a general store at the center...one built just for this community. It'll be boutique, but not high end, and I'll carry a little bit of almost everything."

"Like what?"

I picked up my plan and thumbed through it. Finding the page I sought, I read him the list. "Clothes, office supplies, toys, and hiking gear, for starters. I haven't fleshed it all the way out yet. Maybe books. Maybe even coffee. You know, the idea is to provide all the things we're missing in this market or at the center. Then, if someone wants to open a full store and sell any one of my segments, I'll get rid of it and add the next thing. It's different, but it's resilient. It'll be a shopping experience, fun and profitable, I think. Plus, I'll be there to take some of your workload. You need help. I need an income. The center needs revitalizing. If we can come up with the capital, I can make this work."

Steve beamed.

My intention to open a shop staved my depression and, for the first time in a long time, hope hovered in the air between us. My plan reinvigorated our relationship, stimulated our minds, and got us working together again.

We spent the next eight weeks in a frenzy—remodeling a space, shopping for inventory, doing the paperwork involved in creating a new business—all the while eating less and talking more. The weight came off in fits and starts. Some days, we actually gained a pound or two. Then, almost as if our bodies had held onto the fat for as long as possible, we dropped three. Up and down the scale went, much like my emotions. But in two months we'd each lost over ten pounds.

I want to stress this. *We lost more than ten pounds doing nothing more than sharing meals.*

We still enjoyed our wine or whiskey at night and the occasional dessert. Bread and pasta, beef and bacon remained a part of our diet. We experienced no sense of loss, no great hunger, no longing for food. Instead, we felt fuller. The time we spent together over our meals began to change the shape of our lives.

That change first manifested in the purchase of a teardrop camper and a commitment to play. Our lives revolved around work and our conversations had been limited to business for far too long. We needed more adventure and fun. So, just before I opened my store, we drove to Pensacola, Florida to pick up the camper.

I-40 in October. Tall grass dancing in the wind; trains black and red and rusty against the horizon; chain motels smelling of floral disinfectant and vacuum cleaner dust; clouds casting shadows; billboards selling Jesus; and truckers texting one-handed, eyes on anything but the road.

We held hands until our fingers cramped and let silence soothe us. When the mood took us, our conversations traipsed through politics, love, family, and fears. The drive allowed us to be tourists in our own lives, to see ourselves anew.

At a gas station in Arkansas, I bumped into a woman coming out of the restroom. We both blurted "sorry" at the same time. The long, purple bruise lining her jaw and tear-smeared cheeks made me stop.

I touched her shoulder.

She winced.

"Are you okay?" I asked.

Her eyes darted away from me as she mumbled, "Mind your own business, bitch."

Back in the car, fury competed with hopelessness as I told Steve what I had witnessed. "I don't get it. Why so much violence against women?" We had been talking about the Steubenville rape case and the sentencing of four men in India who had raped a woman to death on a bus.

Steve sighed, shaking his head. "I don't know. Don't these people have daughters and mothers?"

"That's just it. Why do we just have value as daughters and mothers? I mean, it's okay to beat your wife or rape a woman as long as you don't put her in either of the sacred categories? That's just wrong. Why don't we have value by ourselves?"

I raged against the injustice, against my own buried memories of the girl I had been at nineteen. Alone and far from home, I had trusted a man I met in a bar and he violated me. I seldom thought about that night, had put it behind me, but in moments like these, my rage fueled the internal demons that taunted and shamed me. Their voices were a white noise at the edge of my consciousness as familiar as a mother's nagging criticism, and often as inconsequential, until someone or something awakened their full fury. Now, gazing out the bug-stained windows at a landscape shockingly green, the demons hurled noxious taunts and I cringed against them. Eventually, as I held Steve's hand and listened to the hum of his voice, they quieted. In our beat up, gray Blazer, with Steve at the wheel and adventure ahead, I was safe.

We moved farther south into the land of buttered grits, fried catfish, and Waffle Houses. Our discipline relaxed. For Steve, who loves food, the challenge proved almost insurmountable. I heard the refrain, "We're not dieting, right?" too often for my comfort. As he slipped, I slipped, and by the time we arrived in Florida my appetite for fresh oysters and hushpuppies matched his. Guilt crawled across my belly and between my sweat-sticky thighs. The demons woke, their voices a hailstorm of spittle in my mind.

At the beach, I refused to go into the water. Squeezed into my too small bathing suit, I huddled in a cover-up and watched him splash in the waves. When he staggered through the surf and onto the sand, dripping and covered in gooseflesh, he opened his arms to the sky, shook the water from his hair, and grinned. Then he moved to me and I rose to meet him. He grabbed me—the chill of him making me squeal—and kissed me deeply. His mouth tasted of salt and wind and joy. My demons cringed, his love for me a crucifix against them.

The little camper had beach scene stickers, white-walled tires, and bright red hubs. Black Silver Shadow fenders graced its sleek body, their luscious curves reminiscent of big bands and swing dancing. With wood paneling, a queen-sized bed, and a kitchen galley we had to stand outside to use, the tiny teardrop charmed.

In the evenings, we lit candles inside our pop-up tent and savored sultry air, red wine, and Norah Jones singing softly through portable speakers. We divided our days between travel and play, blazing through Alabama and

Mississippi to get to New Orleans—Dixieland on a river boat, the wide river silky in the fading light, the lights of the city jewel-like against an azure sky. On Bourbon Street, every other business seemed to be a strip club. Hawkers sold Jell-O shots, ball caps, and colored beads from every doorway. Jazz standards blared from open-air patios and tourists staggered drunkenly along the sidewalks sipping fruit flavored drinks from tall, plastic cups. Sewage, alcohol, and car exhaust hung in the heavy air while neon signs flashed stenciled breasts and the words "Girls, Girls, Girls." Revolted, we combed the city for a less carnavalistic Jazz scene, found a hole in the wall, and lost ourselves in the passionate music of a trio still willing to give it their all. Faces contorted and dripping with sweat, they made love to their instruments as if we weren't there and, like voyeurs, we reveled in the performance.

Oh, and the food. Crawdad bisque and shrimp Creole, gumbo so spicy it burned our eyes. Cold beer and hot sauce. Chocolate cream pie. As we walked laughing and talking, guilt retreated to a quiet corner in my mind and I reveled in the juicy swish of my too thick thighs.

For ten days, we suspended time. The camper gave us a new found freedom to travel wherever we liked. In Marfa, Texas we chatted with a vendor at the local farmers market and discovered the disdain the locals felt for the rich, New York art collectors who had commandeered their town. On the San Antonio river walk, we watched a duck battle a fish for crumbs, took bad selfies and laughed as we discarded them, fanned our faces with the back of our hands, and finally found shade under a restaurant awning. Over a shared steak and bottle of wine, Steve let his whole self shine. Like a cat getting her belly scratched, I purred at his undivided attention.

On our drives, we drank in wide skies and open landscapes, the expanse calming our busy minds. At a rustic campground in central New Mexico, the clear, calm water of a bottomless lake beckoned. This time, emboldened by romance and adventure, I didn't think twice.

Cool, still water caressed my body, easing cramped joints and stiff limbs. I closed my eyes, shut out the sound of children splashing near the artificial beach, and imagined myself adrift in soft wind and open sky.

4

N eedless to say, I gained four pounds on our trip through the South. Steve gained six. We didn't dwell on it, didn't have time. A week after our return, I opened my store. I had never worked in retail, much less run a retail business, and the ins and outs of making it a success consumed most of my energy. I couldn't fail.

I *wouldn't* fail.

Nights lengthened, the first snows came, and the pre-holiday whirl of retail wore me out. One evening over dinner, I tucked my feet underneath me in pursuit of warmth. We had not yet lit the wood stove and cold crept inexorably through the room. This was the onset of winter, the deadening of the world.

Steve didn't seem to notice the cold. His body burned like a furnace; kept me warm in the wee hours of the night. Instead, he stared at his plate, mesmerized.

"What are you thinking?" I asked.

He looked at me, eyes wide. "I just figured it out," he said.

I put my fork down. "What?"

"It's not about being full. It's about not being hungry."

"What are you talking about?"

He explained that full had always been his goal. He relished the sense of satisfaction and accomplishment when he couldn't eat one more bite. I, on the other hand, didn't really care about food. I ate what was in front of me and enjoyed the flavors, but if left to my own devices would happily live off peanut butter and jelly sandwiches.

"I hate being full," I said.

"Then why do you keep eating?"

"Because it's there," I replied, but that wasn't the whole truth. "Because I don't want to offend you."

Steve shook his head in disbelief. "How would you offend me?"

"If I don't eat what you cook, you might think I didn't like it."

"So what if you don't like it. I don't take it personally. It has nothing to do with me."

I pursed my lips, feeling the conversation slide off course. "Never mind," I said. "It doesn't matter."

He looked at me, forcing my eyes to meet his, and searched my face. Finding something, his mouth softened and he took my hand.

"Honey, you have to know this. I *want* to know what you like and don't like. Your tastes matter. Your opinions matter. I don't want you ever doing things for me that you don't want to do. If you don't like it, I either won't make it or I'll make it for myself and make you something else. It's not a big deal."

My stomach tightened and I looked away. It was a big deal. I had experienced just how big a deal it could be in prior relationships and, in consequence, been well trained. I lived in simultaneous realities, never knowing which would come out on top, always walking the tightrope between. I had been with men who were sweet as could be, but those same men had snapped sometimes, revealing a dark rage that left me cowering in a corner or pinned on a bed before I knew what happened. They had laid the blame on me and I accepted it; was even grateful for it, because if it was my fault, I could do better next time and possibly prevent it happening again.

Steve had never snapped like that, but in my experience most men could. I stole a glance at his face to gauge his sincerity. Worry lined his forehead and his eyes showed concern.

"Okay. Thank you. I'm sorry," I said.

He shook his head again and kissed my hand.

Raised in the sixties by a tough and doting single mom, Steve had learned to respect women and had an unshakeable faith in himself. So, while he knew my history and was sympathetic, he couldn't empathize with me. He had never experienced that sudden, irrational rage or lived with the long-term effects of rape.

It was this that caused our fights. He dealt in logic, fact, and his inalienable right to be himself all the time. I traded in emotion and used lengthy explanations to hint at my truth so I wouldn't trigger an unwanted response. This seldom worked, but I didn't recognize that then. Instead, I just felt misunderstood.

The dogs barked, then bolted to the back door. I got up to let them out and pour another glass of wine. Cold November air hit my cheeks and a thin layer of new snow covered the flagstone patio. Dark hung like fog in the valley below and the warm, fresh scent of manure blew from the barn hidden in its midst. I lingered a moment, settling my heart. When I returned to the table, he had the backgammon board open and the pieces in place. Unlike the one gathering outside the windows, our storm had passed.

"Tell me about not being full," I said.

"Just that. It's enough to not be hungry. I never paid attention to the difference, but it makes sense. If we survived as a species by gorging after a hunt and going hungry when there wasn't anything to eat, then maybe I do that because it's coded in me. But I don't need it. I feel better, lighter, when I don't."

"You look better, too." I laughed.

He poked out his tongue and rolled the dice.

By December, we had lost the weight gained on our trip. Steve had shed thirteen pounds and me eleven, but we were at a standstill. Gift baskets at work filled with baked goods and trays of cookies didn't help. Every morning, the scale said the same thing. We weren't happy about it, but work demanded all our energy. My store exceeded expectations and the Christmas season had me scrambling to find merchandise I hadn't known I would need. Customers and their stories filled my days, shopping online ate up my nights. I raced toward success and was determined to win, but I didn't know the course or where to find the finish line.

Surprisingly, I loved it. I'd gone from the artist's pursuit of deep meaning and quintessential truth to, "Oh my god, that's so cute," and was having more fun than I'd had in years. I hadn't anticipated how much I would enjoy getting to know the people I served or how much I could learn from them. I had worked in solitude for most of the last twenty years, dredging through my experiences and trying to turn them into something of value to the world at large. Now, working in my store revealed that I had value all by myself. Though hard to accept at times, I realized my art wasn't a product I produced. My art was me.

5

In January, our weight continued to fluctuate. Sometimes we magically gained two pounds overnight. This is technically impossible. One might retain weight in water or undigested food, but a body cannot convert calories to fat that quickly.

With the drop in sales after the Christmas rush, I found myself stewing. It had been easy to stay optimistic when business boomed. Now gray days, biting cold, and dismal sales reignited self-doubt. What the hell did I think I was doing? I knew the answer, had expected declining sales, but made it personal anyway. As winter firmed its hold, the depression I had fought to stem deepened, and quiet days surfaced my grief.

Sometimes without warning, tears leaked down my cheeks, the salt-warm sting of them a badge of shame. I had been a bad-ass woman welder, toned and tough, who could throw her man over her shoulder and spin him around without breaking a sweat. These days, I had a hard time lifting a twenty-five pound box. Where demand for my art had kept me constantly scrambling for inventory, I now surfed Facebook, dusted shelves, and bit my lip.

I hid this, of course. When asked about my transition from artist to store owner, I told a half truth. I loved this new business, the interaction with my customers, and the challenge of creating something new and outside traditional models. And yet, I didn't know myself anymore. I had no touchstone that defined me, no place of refuge, no barrier between me and the world. Worry about the business had me trembling inside. Like a small bird in winter wind, I flapped my wings relentlessly and dreamed of a safe place to hide.

Steve shone. His booming laughter and the rapid slap of his feet on the floor preceded him as he moved from one task to another. Proud of the weight he'd lost—twenty pounds now—and his load lightened by my presence at our shopping center, he looked years younger and childlike happy. For him, I could suppress despair. I wouldn't willingly deflate him and his presence buoyed me.

One February afternoon, he came into my store and grabbed me in a giant hug. Lifting me off the ground, he spun me around and kissed me. I laughed as he set me down.

"We haven't been on a date in a really long time. I know we go out, but we haven't had a real date night. I want to take you out," he said.

Late afternoon sun filtered wanly through windows streaked with dust, but the warm lights in my store dispelled winter's gloom. Color bloomed in every corner. Clothing hung tantalizingly from stainless steel racks and the rich aroma of coffee soothed. The corners of Steve's mouth twitched and his eyes sparkled.

"When?" I asked.

"Tonight. Let's book a hotel and go out."

"What do you want to do?"

"Anything." His grin deepened his dimples. "Or everything. As long as it's with you."

We booked a room downtown and left the car with the valet. After checking in, we strolled along San Francisco Street past high-end shops and softly lit window displays. White Christmas lights hung in cottonwoods high above the Plaza and our breath steamed the air.

Still committed to light fare, we stopped at a sushi restaurant known for its unusual tapas and paired our order with hot sake. My fingers tingled from the cold and I took his hand across the linen-covered table to warm them.

"Thank you," I said.

"For what?"

"For this." I gestured to the almost empty room around us.

Candlelight flickered on every table and a red paper lantern bathed the sushi bar in a soft glow. He'd been right. Though we went out often enough, we hadn't made romance the focus of our evenings since our trip across country. Memories of New Orleans Jazz, making love in a camper, and the stillness of a New Mexico lake had dimmed. Since then, evenings out were business related or when we were just too tired to cook.

Steve's undivided attention felt like stepping into a warm bath. I thawed, opening to him and relaxing. When the food came, I sighed deeply. It looked like miniature modern art on a small, white plate. The flavors and textures of Japanese cuisine were strange and exotic. We lingered, sharing tiny bites and holding the sake on our tongues before swallowing, but for all our shrunken appetites it simply wasn't enough food.

Instead of ordering a meal, we left and wandered a few blocks to another tapas restaurant. This one featured the flavors of Spain and we allowed our waitress to make the selections for us. We sat at the bar while she explained the dishes—asparagus and raisin, bacon and fig. The paired sherries she served us danced with the food in our mouths, their movements sensuous and intense. Around us, tables hummed with quiet conversation, the rhythmic murmuring like water in a creek. A musician picked up his guitar and thrummed a Flamenco song.

I shoved my barstool closer to Steve and leaned my head against his shoulder, inhaling his musk—summer light and hayfield sweet. He put his arm around me and stroked my hair.

"Duende," he murmured to the top of my head.

I chuckled. Years before we had attended a performance entitled *Duende*, and had been sadly disappointed. While the performance fell flat, it sparked a discussion about soul, expression, and authenticity. Sometimes we used the word to ridicule those whose expression felt pretentious. At other times, like tonight, we used it to sum up the heightened experience we currently enjoyed.

The music started in my belly and moved quickly to my toes. It stretched my arteries, made my blood run thick and loose, and gummed the back of my throat. I swallowed a sip of something that warmed me like July sun. The sherry vied with the song in carrying me out of cold New Mexico and away from worry and doubt. Tonight, head against Steve's shoulder and smoked paprika in the air, I felt safe and deeply loved.

We meandered out slightly giddy and laughing, unwilling to end the evening. Dessert was next: a lovely orange and chocolate mousse and a large glass of port in yet another nearby restaurant. Finally sated, we made our way back to the hotel.

A band played R&B in the bar and we wormed our way to a table near the stage. We ordered whiskey and took to the floor where gray-haired men played three-quarter time blues to blue-haired women. We recognized the notes of "She Caught the Katy," but struggled to match the unfamiliar tempo.

Steve came close and whispered, "Do you think if I dance faster they'll pick up the beat?"

I snorted as he did just that, his feet moving to the rhythm in his head, but it didn't work. The band just plodded along.

Frustrated, we belted our drinks and headed for the only other place in the area that might offer an opportunity to dance—a dive bar infamous for brawls and the occasional knife fight—a few blocks away on San Francisco Street. On the sidewalk, staggering and giggling, I swerved into him and he put his hand against a wall to stop from falling. He kissed me then, thoroughly, and his warm, generous mouth kindled a flame in my groin.

Almost to our destination, we noticed a bar we'd never seen. A giant glass chandelier hung over a battered wood floor and, behind the bar, an antique mirror reflected bottle backs and hard plaster walls. Deciding to support a new business, we went inside and ordered drinks. As we sipped them, commenting on all the businesses that come and go, a DJ began setting up his equipment. Soon, someone dimmed the lights and a disco ball threw rainbows on the floor. The beat of bass, the pulse of digital fusion, and redundant lyrics made a poem of sound. Stepping into it—into youth, and sex, and muted violence—our bodies moved in disjointed rhythm and we danced like people I didn't know. This was not some rock and roll stick-step. Our liquid bodies moved in all directions simultaneously—a sheen of sweat on neck, and back, and breast—to something we called Hip-Hop, though it was merely house music and, as we learned later, relatively mundane.

At midnight, two of our adult children showed up unexpectedly. The mouth of my eldest son curled in horror when he spied me through the open door. I stepped outside to greet him and he pulled me aside, hissing, "Mom, what the hell are you doing here?"

That was our signal to vacate the bar and we howled with laughter all the way back to the hotel. Later, in our room, Steve pulled me close. When he did, everything between us changed.

6

Dancing became our new passion and we gave ourselves to it completely. Three or four nights a week, we found a band and let loose. A yoga teacher once told me I was so focused on moving forward, I neglected the freedom other directions allowed. Dancing afforded that opportunity. Oh, the joy of it, of closing my eyes and letting the music take me.

At first, we couldn't dance more than one song at a time. Dance one, sit two, dance one, and sit three. My lungs burned and my legs wobbled with the exertion. Sweat poured off my body and plastered the hair to my head. Getting down all the way to the floor proved impossible in the early weeks, but soon we both had the physical strength. On the dance floor, everything melted away—work, doubt, our messy house.

Moreover, the extra pounds rolled off. The scale stopped being fickle. Our libidos leapt. Unlike other forms of exercise, dancing engaged us completely. I didn't spend energy watching the clock and wondering if I had done enough time on the treadmill. Instead, we danced for hours, resenting the breaks between sets. Each night was an adventure as we experimented with new moves and different kinds of music. Hips grinding and bodies shaking to the rhythms, we learned to move together even when dancing apart.

Legs once flabby became taut with muscle, and my stomach—a source of continued shame—firmed so much I was almost proud of it.

People began filming us with their smart phones and college kids called us out, challenging one of us at a time in a how-low-can-you-go, show-me-your-moves kind of thing. We laughed with joy at their bright-eyed grins, loving every moment of it.

By March, I had dropped twenty pounds. Steve had lost thirty. We were more than halfway to our goal and no longer obese. As the weather warmed, my dresses got shorter, my shirts tighter. In an effort to battle the heat of the workout, I shed camouflaging layers of clothing and let my body be seen. Men began to watch me.

At first, I thrilled to the attention. It had been a long time since anyone besides Steve found me sexy. The deliberate intake of breath from a man I passed on the way to the bathroom was a gold star for my accomplishment. I giggled inside when eyes that followed every move I made on the dance floor tracked me back to the table, darting away when I met their gaze. I was visible again, at least when we danced.

In our daily life, however, men stopped looking at me altogether. Steve got compliment after compliment, but people didn't see me. I couldn't figure it out. We'd walk down the hall and they would stop us. "Steve, what are you doing? You look incredible!" Then, as an afterthought, they would glance quickly in my direction and say, "You look nice, too, Destiny."

It took some time to realize that at work I was a wife. On the dance floor, I was an object. In both instances, I didn't exist as an entity in my own right. If men we knew complimented my appearance, they would have to admit they had been looking at my body and that would be an insult to Steve. In a bar, my revealing clothing and sensuous movements invited the attention of strangers. There, Steve got compliments on his moves. I got them on my sexuality. Seldom vocalized, and often creepy, the men made their desires known.

Transfixed, they watched me unabashedly. Their darting glances became deliberate stares. Mouths hung open, tongues licked dry lips. Occasionally, some drunk thrust his hips at me in slimy parody of my moves and I looked away, ashamed of my dancing and body.

I often woke crying from nightmares and suffered unexpected anxiety throughout my days. Driving to work in the mornings, my palms sweated and snakes slithered in my veins. My stomach failed me, lurching and tightening in cramps of pain. I couldn't explain what was happening to me—hadn't made the connection between the men in the bars and my dreams. So I kept quiet and worried I was going insane. The focus on our bodies intensified.

"You are so sexy," Steve said repeatedly.

I wanted to scream, "Stop talking about my body! Stop it! I'm a mind. I'm a heart! I'm not a damned object!" But I didn't. I didn't say a word. Instead, I picked fights.

"Do you think my business is less important than yours?" I asked one evening. We had opened the windows to the warm spring air and a breeze blew a strand of hair across my face. I brushed it away and caught Steve's expression: white edged lips in a tight line and eyes muddied with dread.

"No!" he said.

"I mean it's okay if you do. I just want to know."

He pushed back from the table and stood. "I'm not doing this," he said.

"Oh, great. Walk away like you always do."

And then I followed him, screaming at him for leaving, the anger a momentary release from bodies and the anxiety they create.

Too fat, too thin, just average. Long hair, short hair, high cheekbones, no cheekbones. Pear shaped, card shaped, hourglass. Big breasts, flat chests, the spread of hips. Like most women, I asked "Am I good enough?" a thousand ways each day.

Every woman I know dislikes at least some part of her body. Most can't accept a compliment with grace. We're quick to reassure each other, take comfort in the fact that someone we think is beautiful doubts herself like we do, and compare ourselves mercilessly to each other. We are barraged every day with media images of what we're supposed to look like and messages reiterating the importance of a sex appeal we're not supposed to have if we're good girls.

Looking at myself from a cool, cerebral distance, I knew I was good enough. Hell, I'd proved that time and again, but, like most women, I retained a persistent doubt. Damned if you do and damned if you don't. Women walk a precarious tightrope.

Unfortunately, advertising works and centuries of behavioral practices are ingrained not only in women, but in the men who love them. Knowing something and making the internal changes necessary to disrupt the patterns are two very different things. The war that knowledge created inside me spilled into our lives and though we danced, made love, and laughed with an intensity we hadn't in years, we also fought like never before.

7

We pounded each other with a torrent of angry words. He sat dry-eyed and erect, body quivering with tension. I gathered snatched memories of random events, rendered meaning into them with emotional insistence, and hurled them at him with hot tears coursing down my face.

Inevitably, he left.

His absence ripped my innards, left me hollow, and made a puddle of bleeding-me on the floor. I sobbed uncontrollably, reached for my phone, and called him again and again.

Eventually he answered.

Our fights didn't make sense. As if we spoke two different languages, or lived in different worlds, a barrier existed between us preventing real communication. Half the time I didn't know what we fought about. I only knew I wanted the fights to end, but they didn't. They worsened.

I felt stepped on, overrun, and unimportant. Steve denied my sentiments, vehemently objecting to any accusation I made involving him. He could sympathize with my frustrations at work and in the world, but wouldn't agree he was party to them. He'd seen some of what I experienced daily, but with few exceptions, it hadn't sunk in.

Early in our joint business adventure, I had created an art exhibit space to promote creative economy. Artists showed for free and kept all the revenue from resulting sales. The openings drew our community and brought vibrancy and business to the shopping center. At one opening, a man Steve had known for years pulled him aside.

"This is incredible, Steve." He gestured at the hundreds of people milling through the space. Excited conversation bubbled like a creek, wine flowed, and vibrant art colored tall, white walls. "What a wonderful thing you've done here! What a great idea! This is so important, so necessary."

Steve shook his head and pulled me near. "Let me introduce you to my wife. This is all her. I just pointed the lights," he said.

The man glanced at me when I put out my hand, gave me a quick up and down, and turned back to Steve. "How wonderful of you to support her little projects," he said.

Steve's eyes popped wide and his mouth opened. Dazed, he took my arm and led me away. While this particular occurrence was extreme, it illuminated my daily life. Every time someone praised Steve for my work, the words rendered me inconsequential and exacerbated my distress.

I am the idea person, the marketing wiz, the big picture thinker. He implements. Our combined skills are magic, the sum of them greater than the whole. We did the impossible together, but people either didn't see it or didn't want to know. It wasn't uncommon for people to ask if I did the books or helped organize Steve's office. They assumed he wrote the PR copy, came up with the concepts, and did all the work. When I opened my store, they assumed it belonged to him and he got the credit for its success.

That hurt.

How could I reinvent myself, move past my grief and the loss of both vocation and career, when the efforts I made were invisible? At work, people not only avoided the reality of my body, they ignored my mind. I felt like an appendage, a belonging covertly hidden behind the proud title of wife. While Steve never indulged the praise or accepted the credit, he unknowingly contributed to my angst.

Little things became big in my mind. He read his emails while we shared lunch. Half listening to the story I recounted, he made a phone call and cut off my sentence. He left his trash and paperwork on my sales counter and often interrupted my work.

Normally, the small grievances wouldn't have amounted to much, but this was no ordinary time. The weight loss, new business, and my bottled grief had unraveled a thread and I was coming apart. So, when we fought and he reiterated all the ways he did support and try to give to me, I felt even more invisible, even more unheard.

On the drive back from a buying trip, drained from yet another fight, I tried again.

"I love you and this is killing me," I began.

Steve's hands tightened on the steering wheel and he threw me a sharp look. Deep shadows clung to the hollows beneath his eyes. A muscle ticked in his jaw. "It's killing me, too."

"I know." The fingers of his free hand intertwined with mine and I squeezed them. "Steve, I don't know how to explain in a way that will let you hear me, but I need to matter."

He swallowed and let out a huff of air. "Honey, you *do* matter."

"No, I don't. You make every decision. You—"

"What do you mean I make every decision? *You* make every decision!"

"Don't yell. I'm trying to talk. We *need* to talk."

"I'm not yelling."

"Yes, you are. But I don't want to go there. You do make every decision. You decide where we eat when we go out, which movie we see, what car we drive home."

"Destiny, that's not true. I always ask you what you want to do."

That was true. He did ask, but I knew in my heart that he decided our lives. I just didn't know how to explain it. Out the window, spindly Ponderosas stood like sentries in a yellow meadow. Behind it, the forest thickened, blotting out the sky. The late morning sun hurt my eyes.

"Okay," I sighed. "Never mind."

While our fights had increased in frequency and severity, they never lasted long. Our work lives were so public and intertwined that we had to behave lovingly toward each other during the day. Acting "in love and happy" after a fight made us become loving and happy at night. Besides, we had a hard time staying mad.

A few weeks after our return, we tired of our local bands and decided to try a club in Albuquerque. I wore an outfit I reserved for bigger cities and

Steve matched me. His crisp, collared shirt deepened the blue of his eyes. At a sushi joint, we lamented the still frozen salmon and clumpy rice. Hot sake warmed my mouth as I leaned across the table to kiss him. He put his hand on my bare thigh.

"You look beautiful tonight," he said.

I glanced down, noting the plunge of my neckline, the curve of my breasts lit softly in the candlelight. I felt beautiful, excited, and alive. The anonymity of a strange place emboldened me. Here, if people talked about me behind my back, I would never know. In the morning, I wouldn't bump into someone who had witnessed my moves the night before and have to face judgment or poorly masked desire. The freedom thrilled me.

"Are you ready?" I asked.

He flashed me a grin and stood. "Absolutely."

We walked to the club, Steve's arm curved around my waist. The warmth of his body contrasted sharply with the swish of fabric on my naked legs and a shiver ran up my spine.

In the central room, country music blared from every corner. Plastic cups littered wood tables and Hispanic cowboys in bright boots whirled high-heeled women around the edges of the dance floor, all the couples moving in line. A long-haired kid in his twenties looked me up and down, curled lips revealing yellow teeth and the tip of a bright, pink tongue. I moved closer to Steve and he tightened his grip on my hand.

We passed neon lit bars, a Karaoke stage where a fat and sweating man bleated Elton John, finally making it to our destination. In the far back room, a red dance floor gleamed against black tiles. Dim blue lights and faux leather booths clung to dark walls. I slid into one of the booths and Steve headed to the bar for our drinks. The deep bass of the music reverberated in my stomach. My feet started tapping and my head swayed side to side.

On his return, Steve set down the drinks and grabbed my hand. There were only two other couples in the room and we had the floor to ourselves. Oh, so much room. What luxury to move. I gyrated my hips, moving slow and deliberate against him, and he laughed out loud. The music released us and we reveled in the joy of the dance. Sometimes we danced together, our bodies tight and close. As the tempo increased, we separated, flirting with each other across the floor.

When finally our legs tired, we returned to our table and gulped first water, then whiskey; the burn of it a silk thread down my throat. Sweat crumpled Steve's crisp shirt and his lips glowed purple in the blue light. I pushed a sweaty strand of hair off my face. The bass thumped.

He bent to kiss me, then stopped, glancing up. I turned. A man stood at our table, a bright grin on his face.

"You guys are awesome," he said.

Steve matched his smile. "Thanks."

"I'm Denny. That's my girlfriend, Rose." He gestured to a table on the other side of the room where a plump, pretty woman played with a cup. "If it's okay with you, we'd love to buy you a drink."

Steve glanced at me.

I threw him a look that said, "Why not?"

This kind of thing happened occasionally because, frankly, our dancing was hot and while the attention of single men made me nervous, that of couples did not.

"That would be great, Denny. Thanks," Steve said.

Denny nodded. "What are you having?"

"Jim Beam. Neat."

"I'll be right back."

He returned a few minutes later, cups in hand. Behind him, Rose smiled shyly. I stuck out my hand and we introduced ourselves. They were Native American, with gleaming black hair, proud cheekbones, and rounded shoulders. We warmed to them as they talked and when Denny invited us to dance, we agreed.

They moved well and I enjoyed trading partners for a few songs. Watching Steve dance with another woman gave me a glimpse of what we looked like together and I savored the rare treat. When Denny tired, he stepped off the floor and I moved to follow, but he waved me back and caught Rose's eye. Immediately, she stopped moving. He gestured and she went to him as if caught on a fishing line. They sat down together and he jutted his chin at us with a look that seemed to say, "Keep dancing." So we did.

I twirled toward Steve and he caught me in his arms.

Bending his head to my ear, he said, "What the hell was that?"

"I don't know." A laugh caught in my throat. The exchange had been pretty weird.

We danced another song before returning to the booth. On arrival, we discovered Denny had ordered us another round.

I took a sip and nearly spit it out when Denny said, "Sorry about that. I don't allow her to interact with other men by herself."

"Why?" Steve asked.

"She's my Sub."

"What?" I asked.

"Yes. I'm a Dom and she's my Sub."

Steve compressed his lips and I knew he was fighting to keep his laughter down.

"As in bondage?" I tried not to sound too shocked.

Denny and Rose exchanged a glance.

"Well, sort of," Denny said.

To my chagrin, I had read *50 Shades of Grey* and couldn't help myself. "Um. I've always been sort of curious about that, uh, lifestyle."

Rose grinned and then she and Denny tried to explain it to us. It wasn't like people thought. Every Dom/Sub relationship was different. The relationships, or most of them, were based on respect and shared sexual desires. Sometimes, like in their case, the relationship rules applied outside the bedroom, but the rules were something to which they both agreed.

Steve and I asked question after question, and these articulate, educated people answered them openly. I still couldn't wrap my head around it and when Denny invited us to a party where we could witness variations of the sado/masochist lifestyle first hand, I almost choked.

"Let's dance," I said, grabbing Steve's hand and pulling him up.

On the floor, I moved in close.

"What do you think?" he teased.

"About *what*?"

"Them. The party. Do you want to go?"

I batted my eyes and said, "Well, I don't know. It sounds kind of interesting."

He nodded and I lost myself once again in the dance.

When the song ended, Steve said, "We better get back. I don't want to seem rude."

He led me toward the booth, but halfway back to the table, I stopped. "I need to hit the bathroom. I'll be right back."

"Okay," he said.

On my return, the check had been paid and Steve and Denny were exchanging phone numbers. I hadn't expected that and swallowed hard. We said goodnight to them and made it back to our car with few words between us.

On the drive home, the silence was deafening.

"Um, what was that with the phone numbers?" I asked when I couldn't take it anymore.

"So we can get directions Saturday night."

"Directions?"

"To the party."

I had assumed as much at the club, but needed to hear it from him. "We're *going?*"

"Yeah."

I took a deep breath. "Is this, um, something you want to explore?" I was trying to be tactful, but...Christ! My husband was curious about bondage and I was just finding that out after all these years?

Steve shot me a look. "No. I have no interest in going at all."

I exhaled sharply. "Then why *are* we going?"

A trace of amusement hovered around his mouth, but his eyes were serious. "Because you said you wanted to."

"I did not!"

"You did. On the dance floor."

"Nooo," I said slowly while thinking through the brief conversation I'd thought was just his teasing and my flirting. "I said it sounded *interesting.*"

Steve didn't blink. "Exactly. You said it sounded interesting, so I told them we would go."

And there it was. The thing I had been trying to explain through all our fights and aborted conversations, lit up like a Christmas tree in the predawn of Christmas morning.

"Steve." I paused for emphasis. "I said it sounded interesting. That doesn't mean I want to go."

"But—"

"Honey, listen. I'm interested in bees, but I don't keep them. I'm interested in physics, and engineering, and lots of stuff. It doesn't mean I want to *do* any of them!"

"Saying you're interested and saying yes in that context are the same thing," he said.

"Steve, you assumed something. You do it all the time. You give me a choice and if I say it sounds interesting, you make a decision without asking me if it's what I want to do. We've watched more movies, eaten at more restaurants, and gone places that, had the choice been mine we wouldn't have, because you assume. This is what I've been trying to tell you. You make all the decisions!"

The car slowed as if his thoughts weighed it down. His finger tapped the console between us. Finally, he spoke. "I had no idea. I thought we communicated well."

"*That*," I said, "is another assumption."

8

I never knew losing weight would require me to shed so many other things. As we began to probe the depths of our miscommunication, we discovered its origins proved a bigger threat to our marriage than the fighting ever did.

For years, we had been inseparable: two peas in a pod, two sides of the same coin—all the clichés. We never questioned our compatibility or doubted the strength of our union. Nothing was insurmountable if we tackled it together. Our new revelation opened a crack in that conviction. When Steve demanded I assert myself and tell the truth about what I wanted, I began to be afraid.

After the dissolution of my first marriage, a counselor told me that if one's core remained intact, one could bend in the wind. What she meant, or what I understood, was that I needed to let the little things go. Dining at a second or third choice restaurant didn't damage my fundamental identity. Seeing a war movie rather than the drama I preferred didn't matter, nor did piles on the kitchen counter or socks on the floor.

What I gleaned from our new revelation hinted at the exact opposite. I had allowed him, and the world at large, to inflict a thousand tiny cuts and was bleeding profusely from wounds I refused to see.

When he asked what I wanted for dinner and I said I didn't care, I diminished my health. When I cleaned up after him, I wasted time that should have been mine. Still, I clung to my old narrative and pretended everything was fine. Women are supposed to be compliant. They are supposed to be resilient. They are supposed to put family (or husbands) first.

While I could be a strong woman, even powerful, I was still a woman and that meant overlooking things to keep the peace. But weight loss is about more than food. Eating less made a good beginning. Adding the dancing accelerated the endeavor. Now the process demanded something more, because success requires a fundamental shift in all aspects of life.

I began in the safest possible way. Before I met Steve, I had been a strong advocate for organic foods. When we merged homes, his children balked at granola, healthy snacks, and homemade spaghetti sauce. They wanted Lucky Charms, soda, and jarred Alfredo. While they appreciated my cooking, they resented the imposition of my will on their lives. I had decided it wasn't worth the fight.

Now, children grown and out of the house, I took the first steps toward self-assertion by changing how we shopped. Instead of stopping nightly at our local grocer, we made a weekly trip to town and stocked up on healthy foods. We snacked on carrots instead of chips, and I started packing our lunches.

A large mixing bowl of salad greens, artichoke hearts, roasted red pepper, beets, avocado, and sunflower seeds contains approximately 900 calories. When dressed with the juice from the artichokes, beets, and peppers, it is delicious and enough to comfortably feed us both. I cut out the bread, replacing it with rice cakes, and eliminated all processed food from our diet.

My skin cleared. Aching joints quieted. I could dance longer and harder and not be so tired the next day. Instead of watching Steve cook at night, I joined him and we made our meals together. New recipes rekindled my delight in food while accelerating the weight loss. Breakfast became a protein shake instead of fried eggs. Dinner might be lamb one night, but the next it would be stir fried vegetables or lentil stew. Better food proved more satisfying and more nutrients meant fewer calories. Our enjoyment of this change empowered me to assert my preferences in other small ways.

"Please don't leave your paperwork in my store" felt safe. "Please don't hold your meetings in my store" didn't. That was too big a leap this soon. Steve responded gracefully to requests related to his understanding of himself. He owned his chaotic messiness. He didn't, however, respond well to new or unexpected criticism. In his mind, he included me as a partner when he held court in my arena. To tell him differently might provoke defensive wrath or, worse, cold disdain.

Occasionally, I expressed my desire to watch a particular movie and he acquiesced. In those moments, I experienced incredible guilt. I knew what it was to sacrifice for someone I loved and didn't want to inflict even one of those thousand tiny wounds.

They say that marriage is compromise. It isn't, or at least not in the way commonly understood. Compromise doesn't mean taking turns or squishing yourself down for your partner's well being. It's about personal responsibility, mutual respect, and finding things you enjoy doing together. While we shared the respect, neither of us was particularly good at personal responsibility.

Steve held meetings in my store because of its pleasant environment and lack of clutter. His own office was stacked high with debris and instead of cleaning it, he did that portion of his business in my store, bringing his debris along. A half full cup of coffee always landed on my sales counter. Bills stacked up on my coffee counter. A computer languished against my wall. His booming voice drowned out conversations with my customers. Sometimes, whilst I conducted a sale, he slipped in behind me and commandeered my computer, leaving me unable to work after the customer left.

Outwardly, I smiled. How could I embarrass him in front of his client or business associate by asking him to leave? Was it really a big deal to give up my computer for a few minutes? I felt petty, but inwardly seethed. My lack of personal responsibility prohibited me from voicing frustrations. I didn't want to be a nagging or intolerant wife. I trembled at how he might interpret my protest and didn't want to face his reaction.

Steve dealt with unpleasant situations by either leaving or issuing black and white ultimatums. I imagined him telling me, "Fine. Then I won't come into your store again." The thought made me panic. Of course I wanted him around, wanted snatched kisses and shared interactions throughout the day. I didn't know how to scale the walls he put up when

I displeased him or express my needs in a way that would mitigate his displeasure. The last thing I needed was to spark another fight, so I practiced assertiveness in small ways and focused on the things I did right.

Those things formed a list in my head and became a security blanket, something to cling to when vulnerable and afraid. My business had made it through the first quarter without bleeding. That, by itself, seemed a miracle. My children had grown into people I adored—a surprise after the difficult teen years—and they sparkled in my life. Steve and I would celebrate our tenth anniversary in a few months and our love burned in me, dragon-like.

Count your blessings. Don't sweat the small stuff. Don't take anything personally. Be here now. The litany of popular psychology bombarding my Facebook page promised happiness and I embraced it, rattling off my blessings like beads on a rosary and praying for peace of mind.

9

eace proved elusive. In a conversation over brunch on a lazy, Sunday morning, Steve blamed his excessive weight on me. The words I wanted to hurl at him stuck in my throat like a clump of soggy, white bread and I drained the rest of my lukewarm tea.

"*What?*" I asked.

"It's true. You didn't like me flirting with other women when we first met and that's why I got fat."

"You flirt all the time. With men and women. It's who you are."

Steve crossed his legs and began picking at the dry skin on his feet. Little shreds of it fell to the floor, a dusting of snow on our red wool rug.

"You're wrong," he said mildly.

"I am not. You hug people all the time. You banter with them. You turn on your charm and they circle around you, moths to a flame."

He laughed. "So do you."

"Okay, but that's not what we're talking about here. Explain."

"I told you about my mom, right? How she didn't want to date after she and my dad separated?"

I thought about it, about her, and nodded. "Yes, but what does that have to do with me?"

"You used to get jealous and I did what she did. I used the weight to keep women away. If they don't see me as sexy, they won't flirt with me and I won't flirt with them."

"That's ridiculous. I wasn't jealous. I've *never* been jealous."

Steve shook his head. His jaw drooped almost mournfully and his tone of voice shifted as if he spoke to a child. "Do you remember that time at the basketball game when you got so pissed off at me?"

I flushed, the heat of that moment burning my cheeks. "I got pissed because you disappeared for half the game and left me cheering the kids by myself. You were so engaged with that woman, you ignored all of us completely. That wasn't me telling you not to flirt. It was me telling you that I resented your absence."

"You were jealous," he said again.

I took a deep breath, let it out slowly through my nose, and closed my eyes. I wouldn't fight about something that happened almost ten years ago and wouldn't let him derail our conversation.

"It doesn't matter. If you feel that way, feel your weight gain happened because I was trying to restrict you somehow, then that needs to change. I'm sorry you misinterpreted me." I took his cracked, ink stained hands in mine. "Honey, I love you. I don't want to inhibit you in any way. If you want to flirt, flirt. I mean it. Don't ever shrink for me."

He chuckled and patted his belly. "I am shrinking for you. Should I stop?"

"Ugh! That was a terrible joke. No, don't stop that."

I rose, picked up our plates, and kissed him on the top of his head. The lingering aroma of laundry detergent from a freshly washed pillow case clung to his sleep flattened hair.

Over the next few weeks, while I practiced being assertive and portioned our food, Steve paid new attention to his appearance. Instead of stained tees and baggy jeans, he donned collared dress shirts and ensured his jeans were clean. He got a hair cut, shaved every day, and said it was all for me.

For the first time since I'd met him, Steve looked the role he played. A glimpse of him walking down the hall caught my breath and a voice in my head whispered, "That's *my* man." With a long, straight nose and high forehead, strong chin and sparkling eyes, he cut through a room like John Travolta on a dance floor: fluid, graceful, and bigger than life. I wasn't the only one who noticed. Women sang his praise in my store. They hugged him a little longer than necessary and twittered like birds when he gave them his time.

It made me grin to watch him bloom, his light growing full and bright. When he whirled me on the dance floor and I caught someone's admiring gaze, I once again felt safe. People weren't just looking at me; they were looking at us. We were *that* couple and the knowledge gave me pride.

One night, after a drink and several glasses of water, I stepped away from the music to stand in the restroom line. Steve kept dancing. He flashed me a smile when he spun in front of me, then closed his eyes; hips shaking, feet sliding, hands moving up and down his sides. Lost in his own world, his beauty stopped my heart.

When we first started dancing, we couldn't get enough of each other and sex had been great, but as my business and the discipline of dancing took their toll, our libido had waned. Most nights, we didn't have the energy to engage. Tonight, watching him move without me, I wanted him badly.

By the time I made it into the bathroom, I thought my bladder would explode. Women still occupied the two small stalls and I crossed my legs like a child. Sweat trickled down my back and between my breasts. The clean, healthy scent of it mingled with urine, perfume, and air freshener in the tiny, graffiti covered room. For the millionth time, I wondered why women took so long to pee. Finally, a stall door opened and I sidled past a large woman in a tight shirt, urgency making me rude. She huffed at me and I murmured an apology as I hurried inside.

Out of the bathroom, I shoved my way through the crowd and back to our table. Steve wasn't there. I scanned the room, didn't find him, and turned toward the dance floor. Bodies shimmied and swayed in a sensuous tapestry of color, shape, and line. At first, I didn't see him. Then my stomach lurched. Wedged into a corner near the stage, Steve danced slow and sexy with a woman I didn't know.

Her tight, tiny body moved in rhythm with his. His big hand covered the small of her back. He leaned close and said something. She laughed. I watched as he released her, twisted his hips, and sunk low. His chin hovered at her crotch and she gyrated for him, her motions deliberate. Though the heaving room was too hot, my skin went cold. I sat, heavily, before my legs gave out.

"Think," I told myself. "Don't react. Just think."

It didn't help.

Every instinct said this was more than a casual dance. I gulped air, trying to slow my heart, then slammed my whiskey. Its burn settled my nerves a little. Steve was loyal. He would never cheat. This was harmless and probably not what I feared. Relaxing slightly, I watched them move. When the song ended, they parted. Twisting my neck against the tension, I took to the floor again and our evening resumed.

10

I couldn't stop thinking about her, though. In my dreams that night, I saw the silky sheen of her black hair swinging free past her shoulders, the dark gleam of it an insult to my own mousey brown locks. Steve reached out a hand, pushed a stray tress out of her face, and bent to kiss her. Then the dream narrative careened in another direction. A man's hands groped at my jeans. A hand throttled my neck. I couldn't breathe to scream. I woke, writhing and afraid.

"What's wrong," Steve asked when I staggered to the couch in the morning, slit-eyed and frowning.

"Bad dream."

"Tell me."

I crawled on top of him, nestling my head into his shoulder. "It's nothing. Just hold me," I said. Unwilling to appear jealous after our recent conversation, I didn't want to talk.

He pushed.

I caved.

"Who was that woman you were dancing with last night?" I tried to keep my voice neutral and failed.

Steve tensed, then relaxed. "I think her name is Laurie. She's a realtor in town. What was your dream?"

"You were kissing her."

"Honey, it was a dream. I would never do that." He pulled me tighter, stroked my hair, and kissed my neck.

I felt the fool. I had given him permission to flirt and it had just been a dance. Shaking off the mood, I rose to make tea and our day began.

We took a leisurely shower and I applied makeup while he shaved. As he gathered loose change, car keys, and his wallet off the dresser, a card fell off and fluttered to the floor. I stooped to retrieve it.

"Do you need this?" I asked. Steve's pockets were always filled with debris and trash often mingled with necessary items. I was accustomed to picking up folded papers, old receipts, and the business cards thrust upon him each day.

He glanced at the card in my hand, then snatched it from me and stuffed it in his pocket. "Yes. That's the realtor's card," he said.

Worry niggled my stomach. "She gave you her *card*?"

"I'm going to show her the warehouse in town. She might have someone interested in it."

I thought back to the previous night. I hadn't been gone that long. When did he have the opportunity to open a dialog with her? Hell, when did she give him her card?

Turning so he wouldn't see my face, I reached for my dress.

"Who's interested?" I asked.

"She won't say until she's seen it."

"When are you going to show her?"

He sat on the bed and pulled on his shoes. "I don't know. I'm going to call her today."

Alarm bells rang in my head, reverberated through my body, and made me sweat. I risked a quick look at him and his blank face silenced my fear. Stop it, I told myself. Just stop it.

We finished dressing, fed the dogs, and went to work. Between customers, restocking, ordering, and the incessant Facebook crawl for relevant posts, I put the woman and her card out of my mind. At lunch, Steve and I spoke of ordinary things. A new tenant delayed her opening. The janitorial service wasn't performing. The water line might have a leak. By dinner that night, I had all but forgotten about the woman.

She called him as I poured the wine. At first, I didn't realize who was on the line because his voice went slippery and smooth like it did when talking with a stranger. Clients called at seven in the morning and nine at night. They had an uncanny knack for interrupting almost every meal. He always answered, and I could tell by his tone if he was speaking with someone old or young, male or female. It amazed me how comfortable he made people feel.

This call was different. Instead of leaning back in his chair, he paced back and forth between the couch and dining table like he did when resolving a particularly difficult problem or consulting with someone on a deal. Pots simmered noisily on the stove behind me and I couldn't hear what he said. I studied him, trying to discern the subject of the conversation. Anticipation lit his face and his eyes gazed past me at something I couldn't see. Finally, he moved back into range.

"Thursday at eleven? Great. That'll be great. I'll see you then," he said.

After he set his phone on the table, I handed him a glass of wine and asked, "Who was that?"

"What?" he asked, still focused. Then he shook his head slightly, as if clearing his vision. "Oh. That was the realtor from the other night. I'm going to show her the building on Thursday."

I nodded, glad of it and well past my earlier funk. Leasing the warehouse would take a lot of pressure off us both. While my business was doing well, I still wasn't drawing an income and the financial hit had been hard.

"I've got staff on Thursday. Do you want me to come?"

Steve started. "Uh, no. I mean, you can if you want to, but this isn't a big deal. I'm just showing it. I don't want to pull you out of your store for that."

I had wished for a different answer, but changed the subject as we sat down to dinner.

"Did you know the size of dinner plates has increased more than twenty percent since 1900 and portion sizes have increased thirty-six percent since the eighties?"

Steve put down his fork. "Really?" he asked.

"Yep. The bigger the plate, the more people will put on it and the more they'll eat. Don't you think that's gross?"

Contemplating his bowl, he nodded. "Makes sense, I guess. Think about large cokes. Christ, they're huge. Like who needs that much sugar? I'll have a burger and a side of diabetes, please."

"Two hundred and fifty percent bigger than the regular size. It astounds me. No wonder the country's obese." I took a bite, savoring rich spices and the nutty texture of quinoa.

"I like eating like this so much better," Steve said around a mouthful of turkey sausage. "It still surprises me. I really thought I would miss the crap."

"Do you miss it at all?" I asked.

"No. I really don't."

"Then I have a question for you."

He finished the last bite and licked the bowl with his finger. "Shoot."

"Do you think you could give up sugar?"

Steve pulled his finger from his mouth and sucked the last bit of flavor from his lips. "I don't know," he said. "I can try. Why?"

"Because it's terrible for us, and it's addictive, and I just think it would be good for us."

Steve had yet to control all his urges. He bought candy in huge bags to refill the machines at work, grabbed a handful every time he walked by them, and often emptied them in the process. I hated seeing that and did worry about diabetes, but since we weren't technically dieting, I had hesitated to bring it up.

"Think you can give up Cherry Garcia?" he said.

"Oh. I don't know. I hadn't thought about *that*." I laughed. "But if it's good for the goose, then it's good for the gander. Right?"

Steve smiled and said, "Let's give it a try."

11

The following Thursday dawned bright. A cool, blue sky backed pine covered hills and I gazed at them, missing the honey in my tea. It tasted thin and bitter, but 60 calories was 60 calories and I tried not to blanch. Steve took a sip and made a face.

"We have to give up honey, too?" he asked.

"We have to break our addiction to sweet. We can bring it back later."

He smacked his lips together a few times, exaggerating the sound, and I rolled my eyes. "Just a few days, and then it'll be okay. At least that's what the Internet says."

"What's your day look like?" he asked.

"Usual. I don't think I've got anything special on the schedule. How about you?"

"I've got that meeting with the realtor."

I'd forgotten about that and its mention squeezed my chest a little. "Sure you don't want me to come?"

"No. I'm good."

"Okay," I said. "Will you be back in time for lunch?"

Steve nodded, a large bite of melon in his mouth. The sweet fruit soothed my palate, erasing the bitter tea residue, and we ate in silence for a minute. Finally, he pushed his plate aside.

"Yeah. It shouldn't take long. I'm going to head straight to town and get some errands out of the way before I meet her, but I should be back by one."

I squelched a sigh and felt my shoulders relax. "Great. Call me when you're done."

He seemed distracted as he gathered parts to a computer he had worked on the previous night; so distracted that I had to stop him for a kiss before he made it out the door. The quick kiss was thin as the bitter tea and it hollowed me. When he left, the door closed behind him like a slap. The silence of the house descended around me and I hurried through the rest of my morning routine.

I rang his phone at 1:15. It went to voicemail. By 1:30, nerves competed with hunger and my belly clenched. An hour passed. I called again. He didn't answer. Feeling disconnected from the earth, my body like vapor, I slowly served a portion of the salad I had made and sat down to eat. I couldn't taste the food. Water didn't ease the dryness in my mouth. Why hadn't he called? What was taking so long?

First, I worried. Then, I raged.

Steve showed up a little past three. I couldn't look at him, kept my face to the computer screen, and clenched my teeth to stop the torrent of accusations I wanted to hurl. He spun my chair around and his exaggerated grin faded.

"My phone died," he said.

"I thought you said it wouldn't take long."

"We went for lunch. She wanted to talk about some things."

"And you couldn't call me?" I seethed with a rare fury, but kept my voice cold.

"I told you. My phone died."

"What? *Laurie* didn't have one you could borrow?" I asked, stringing out her name so it sounded lewd and crass.

He stiffened visibly.

Through our children's teen years, they had all used this excuse when breaking curfew or not being where they were supposed to be. Each time one of them did, Steve had pointed out the fallacy. Everyone had a phone. At any point they could have borrowed one and staved our worry. As excuses went, that one was lame.

"I'm sorry. I didn't think of it."

Turning my back to him, I tried unsuccessfully to control my trembling hands. He walked away, his footsteps punctuation marks pounding in my brain.

Steve didn't speak to me for the rest of the day and by the time I got home my anger had mellowed to meekness. He pretended nothing had happened and we spent the evening in front of the TV, neither of us willing to break the tenuous thread holding our fight at bay.

Through the next few weeks, I kept my fears to myself. He met with her again; another lunch in town, another meeting at our center, back to the warehouse, and who knows where after. But I knew him. He wouldn't cheat.

Would he?

Scouring the Internet for articles on marriage, recovering from an affair, and what men need only confused me. Jumbled thoughts collided in my head like carnival lights—too loud, too fast, too many all at once. My anxiety worsened. Dizzy spells, nausea, and blinding headaches plagued my days. Fingers slick with sweat fumbled on the keyboard. My once sharp memory gave way. Nightmares tore at my sleep and I woke lethargic as if I'd been drugged.

"Please, God," I prayed. "Don't abandon me."

When we danced, I watched him covertly. Was he looking at other women? Dancing out of character? Paying attention to anyone but me? No, I concluded. Everything felt the same.

Then, one early morning well before dawn, I woke again from the same horrible dreams. I reached for him and found him gone. Shaking, I made my way to the couch and glanced at his computer screen. At the top of the page, a box flashed the word Incognito. A wave of dizziness took me to my knees. By the time he reached me, my tears leaked. I couldn't stop them, couldn't speak.

12

Steve pulled me into his arms, but I scarcely felt him. Blood made wind in my ears, made his garbled voice the movement of trees.

Incognito.

God, what is he hiding from me?

I had lost my first husband to the Internet. Our often dubious union collapsed completely as that flickering screen sucked him out of my life and into a dark world filled with needy people and anonymity. Now, again, the computer's seductive hum sung a siren song to the man I loved. Past and present collided. My steel heart screamed as it bent and tore, ripping me to pieces until Steve held the mangled remains of someone I thought had ceased to be.

Feeling returned first to my cold, cold feet. He said nothing, just rocked me. Gradually, I felt the warmth of his body pressed tight against my back, his breath on my cheek, and our tangled legs in an uncomfortable heap. I made move to rise, and he helped me up and led me gently to the worn blue couch; its familiar sag a cradle. The blanket he tucked around me smelled of old dogs and dust, but it was soft. Slowly, I returned to reality.

Steve sat beside me and grabbed my arm. "Oh, God! Destiny! Are you all right? Honey? Please. What happened?"

I wiped my cheeks with the backs of my hands, ran moist fingers through my hair, and took a shuddering breath. Then I gestured at the computer screen. "Incognito, Steve? Really? That's where we are?"

Hope drained through me like water through a sieve and my limbs were the dead weight of misery.

"What?" he asked, turning sharply to follow my gaze.

"That. You've got the browser on Incognito." I shook my head slightly in disbelief. My nostrils flared in disgust and spilled pooled snot. I wiped it away.

Steve's eyes went wide. "Incognito? I don't even know what that means."

I was too drained to fight and too startled by his expression to do more than explain.

We spent the next several hours talking, arms crossed and rigid, staring at each other over steaming cups of tea. He laid out his facts like pebbles—round, small, and perfect—but pebbles don't make a rock, and a rock was the only thing I could see.

Ultimately, he convinced me he hadn't cheated. Facts—phone records, emails, hours in the day—remained meaningless. His haunted face, open body, and hands clutching his cup to refrain from gripping me were the things I believed. Perhaps I shouldn't have, but I did. My faith in him had been shaken, but this was still the man I knew.

And yet something was very wrong. In my heart, Steve had betrayed me. Except he hadn't and I didn't have the words to express my conviction. It all felt so very real. I too could line up a series of pebbles and create a truth as plausible as the one he professed. My truth took its roots in threat. Fear clung to me, sharp-toothed and hungry. Every time I tried to name its source in our fights, in my head, the driver of my emotions retreated shadowlike into the dark.

I shared my bed with a stranger. Now hard-boned and muscled, Steve no longer resembled my husband. A clavicle replaced the soft tissue that had given to my weight. As my arms encircled his frame, his smallness made me unsafe. Men's eyes watched me all the time. The mirror reflected my shame.

By this time, I had lost thirty-four pounds. Steve had lost sixty. I could see the changes in my body, but they seemed insignificant. I still had stretch marks from hell. Welding scars marked my hands and forearms in a crisscross of tiny, white lines. Above my knees, aged skin sagged. That woman with whom Steve had danced was fifteen years younger than me. No crinkles worried her eyes. No flesh wobbled on the underside of her toned, tanned arms. No matter how much weight I shed, I would never again be that young.

My customers and I decorated our bodies. Bold leggings under layers of loose clothing shrouded our perceived imperfections. We looked for statement pieces that expressed our uniqueness without drawing unnecessary attention to our flaws. Every day, women bemoaned their bellies, hips, and hair as they tried on clothes. Outwardly, I denounced their lament. To me, they were all beautiful, extraordinary even. They inspired me, taught me, made me laugh; but while I bolstered them, I criticized myself.

Steve, on the other hand, seemed to glide on air. He danced in the hallways at work, dimples deepening with mirth every time someone laughed at him. The grace of his body, the light in his eyes begged a running stream of questions. "What did you do? What diet are you on? God, you look great!"

He always replied in the same way. "Well, we invented something new. It's called eating right and exercise." They didn't believe him. "No. Really. It's not a diet. We're just sharing meals and dancing," he said.

They sighed, then said, "It's so romantic. That's why it's working. You're doing it together." Or, "I'd like to do this with my wife."

Weight loss is usually associated with deprivation and we've all seen the pinched faces of those on strict dietary regimens. There's a particular tightness around their mouth and eyes. They may be dogged, and worthy of our applause, but they don't glow. Steve did and, in his company, so did I. Together we inspired.

Couples and individuals took our advice. Our banker lost 10 pounds. A couple bicycled across the patio and the woman called to me. "We don't dance, but we can ride bikes." At work and on the dance floor, at a restaurant or hiking our favorite trail, I didn't brood. Worry and fear dominated only my private hours, my dead of night. While I chatted with customers, flirted with Steve, and stayed busy, I was happy. Our public life warmed us. In private, however, the tiniest thing could trigger a fight. I was Jekyll and Hyde.

Though I had retracted my accusation that he was having an affair, it sat heavy between us. He did what he could to dispel any lingering doubts, but his efforts made me more uneasy. Every time he called me sexy, I cringed inside. Our little trailer sat idle in the driveway and dancing became a chore.

In less than eight months, I had lost my career and identity, opened a store, published a third book, dropped thirty-four pounds, and radically shifted my perception of my marriage. Squeezed by change, plagued by unexplained fear, and exhausted from late nights, I began to crack.

13

July came. Monsoon rains, sweltering days. The high desert choked on the dry, bittersweet scent of flowering chamisa. I shivered in the store's air conditioning and longed for the sight of my dogs running free, the cool of a pine forest, the relief of a creek. I didn't get it.

Instead, the owner of the only hardware store in our area shared her retirement plans with me. She suggested we buy her assets and open a new store in our center. It was an incredible opportunity. With butterflies in my stomach, I presented the possibility to Steve.

"We have to do it," I said.

"If we don't, someone else will," he agreed.

A hardware store would be our cinch pin, the anchor our center had always needed.

"Downside?" I asked.

In his undersized shop, computer skeletons and green bits of broken RAM littered the floor. Wires hung like tangled hair from his workbench. The buzzing of hundreds of lavender drunk bees drifted through the open door.

Steve leaned back and patted his almost flat belly meditatively. "Well, space for one. Where would we put it?"

Over the next few weeks, we honed a rough plan. The old hardware store would close by the end of September. We would have to be open in early October or our potential customers would get used to shopping in town. Cash was limited and time was short. If we did this, it could make or break us. As Steve began his obsessive research, I put a caveat on the project.

"Hey, love, just one thing," I said.

He stopped crunching numbers and looked at me. "Okay. What?"

"Promise me we won't give up our time."

The delicate peace between us required me to speak my mind and him to take at least one day off each week so we could spend daylight hours together outside work. That time kept me grounded and somewhat sane. I wouldn't give it up.

Steve shoved his papers aside and kissed my hand. Soft eyes met mine, deep with love and sadness. I winced at their nakedness. The terrible fights had made our current happiness fragile.

"I promise," he said.

My heart swelled with relief. "God, I love you. You know that?"

We didn't just agree to buy the remaining assets from the existing hardware store; we bought assets from four more. An auction in Missouri left us bruised, filthy, and sore, but the drive there and back was balm to our emotional wounds. Towering oaks in full leaf sated our need for green. A flock of birds swooped low over cornstalks and ponds shimmered in afternoon light. Telephone wires and trains. The relentless billboards again. We brought a cooler along so we wouldn't have to eat road food. While he drove, I fed him bites of avocado and cheese. Holding hands, we listened to audio books and the long drive calmed my jangled nerves. Several nights without dancing let me catch up on my sleep. I didn't think about how I looked, Steve flirting, or hungry eyes.

Steve was an auction pro, but this was my first experience and I thrilled to it. In this world, skill and preparation competed with the bargain hunter's lust and I excelled at the dance of nuance, gesture, and presence of mind.

Building the hardware store brought us closer. We reveled in the planning, scheming, and hard work. Together again, in synch, and harmonious, our initial endeavors exhilarated us. Steve hit his weight goal and I wasn't far behind. We celebrated, and I monitored our calorie intake closely. Now, he needed to eat more than me. To keep sharing meals in the same way, I brought him protein bars and other snacks throughout the day. Minutes ticked into weeks and our vicious deadline loomed, a cloud on the horizon threatening heavy rain.

Thousands and thousands of tiny parts had been crammed into white, plastic trash bags. They filled every inch of space in a two thousand square foot room. Sorting them, erecting shelving, and finishing construction while hiring staff, setting up wholesale accounts, and running three other businesses proved daunting if not downright impossible. Steve went into overdrive. Time off sputtered and died.

We had wildly underestimated the scope of the project. Often our days began at three in the morning and ended well past midnight. On the rare occasion we found ourselves home of an evening, we were too tired to talk. Instead, we'd plop in front of the TV and wake in the wee hours to stagger disoriented to bed. Pulled in too many directions at once, the stress wore on us both.

Discipline and promises are similar. Under stress, they are difficult to maintain. For months, we had scorned pizza. A burger had been a rare treat. Now, with neither time nor energy to cook, they became staples in our diet. Like alcoholics in trauma, we fell off the wagon in every conceivable way. The work replaced dancing. In our rush to get the job done, our long, lingering meals disappeared and we ate feverishly. The closer we got to opening day, the sharper Steve became.

"Hey, babe, I need you to take a look at the t-shirt design," I said.

"Not now!" he replied.

I backed away. "Steve, we're at deadline on the signs. You have to decide on the color."

"Later!" he almost screamed.

His graceful steps became staccato stutters as he raced to and fro. A knot formed in my stomach and set up camp for a long stay. Terse exchanges in snatched moments moved us forward, but not fast enough. I retreated from his shrill, snapping voice and tense, white face. So much for speaking my mind.

Trying to mitigate his stress, I took on more responsibility. Tasks that should have been his fell into my lap and it was either do them or let the project fail. Simultaneously, my business was gearing up for the holiday season. We couldn't afford to put money into it if it didn't pull off the holiday sales.

One afternoon in early September, I had carved out time to meet with an important sales rep. Many of her lines were critical to my holiday success. We went through the catalogs and samples as quickly as possible because a mountain of work buried my desk. Steve came in, planning to meet with his True Value representative. Seeing us, he grimaced and left. About twenty minutes later, one of his staff interrupted me.

"Destiny, I'm sorry to bother you, but I need—"

"I'm sorry. I'm in a meeting. You'll have to find Steve."

"I did. He says he's too busy and to ask you."

The air went out of me. What the man needed was important and couldn't wait. I apologized to my rep, dealt with the problem, and returned to my meeting, seething.

That night I worked up my nerve and confronted Steve over dinner.

"I really didn't appreciate you sending your staff to interrupt my meeting."

"I didn't have a choice. My meeting was too important."

"And mine wasn't?" I asked.

"What? You're meeting with someone who's trying to sell you something and I'm trying to get this damn store open. What would you have me do?"

I allowed the possibility that I was being petty. "What was your meeting about?"

"The opening stock order. I have to get it in by next week or we won't have product to open."

"Let me ask you a question. What happens if I don't have product for Christmas?"

He looked at me blankly. The thought had obviously never crossed his mind.

I shook my head and took a gulp of wine. "Okay, I'll tell you. If I don't have product for Christmas, it really won't matter if the hardware store opens on time. My business will fail. There's not enough money in the bank to keep it afloat and do the hardware store too. So you see, while you were working on a critical order, so was I. And Steve, I really resent that you made my business less important than yours. Hell, I resent that you make my time less important than yours."

He appraised me like he would a particularly nasty bug, red-rimmed eyes sharp and cold.

"God *damn* it, Steve! I need to matter!" I cried. If I couldn't have his touch or our time together, I would at least have his respect.

Our fight raged most of the night.

14

Steve wanted me to be assertive, to express my needs and desires like he did, but it seemed those needs and desires only mattered when they didn't directly interfere with his priorities. I demanded his respect, but proved unworthy of it because I didn't respect myself. I could have told his employee no and accepted the consequences, but I didn't.

Why?

Him, me, us; it was all such a tangled mess. I often wondered what it would be like to be Steve. I could call him self-absorbed, but was he any less so than me?

Confidence was the real difference between us. If he angered me, he didn't worry about terrible outcomes. He never walked quickly through a dark parking lot. I imagined living in a world where I could appreciate a stranger's admiring glance without automatically gauging his level of threat. There were so many subtle variations in our day-to-day experience.

At one point during this period, a man came into my store and asked me to carry his books and CDs. I declined, citing lack of room. In truth, his products weren't a good fit, but I didn't want to hurt his feelings. Rather than accepting my decision with grace, he examined the store's layout.

"How about there, in the corner?" he asked.

"I'm sorry. If I put a rack there, it would block my light."

He argued, vehemently enough that I proved it to him. Why I did this was beyond me at the time.

"Well there, then." He gestured to a small bookshelf holding the work of local authors. "My stuff will sell way better than that." As he said this, he took a step toward me, placing his body inches from mine.

My hackles went up. "That's pretty arrogant of you," I replied. Heart beating fast, I retreated to the safety of my sales counter.

He followed, insisting I do what he said.

Finally, I'd had it. "Look. I don't want to insult you, but if you'll take a look around, you'll discover your products don't belong in my store. That's it. End of conversation."

His face mottled and went red. He clenched his fists. I saw his jaw work and thought he would say something. He didn't. He just left. All day, I worried about him. Would he be waiting for me in the parking lot that night? Or maybe the next?

Steve didn't live with physical intimidation or condescension. Nobody diminished the work he did or rendered him invisible with their attitude. What would that feel like? What would it be like to truly be free? At home and at work, I held our relationship as my top priority. He took our union as a given, and though he remained sensitive to my needs, he put them aside when necessary. He loved me. He meant it. But this was life.

I couldn't be so casual, so trusting. When I'd made my own money, things had been different. Then strong enough to easily lift two hundred pounds, I seldom questioned my safety. Now I felt frail and needed him more than he needed me. I did his work and our domestic chores to be indispensable and worried he would eventually replace me. But it was too much. My dandelion-like tenacity for self-preservation demanded a change.

The cold dawn following our fight glittered on the tile floor. My body ached. Hot tea sent whirls of fragrant steam into the air in front of me. Voice hoarse from too many tears, I whispered, "I'm sorry."

I was. Not for what I wanted from him, but for the dissolution of our lives, the hurt and haggard lines around his eyes. We were coming apart at the seams. He had broken his promise by compromising our time and had been an asshole to me and everyone around him, but our argument had nothing to do with that.

"You can't have it both ways, you know," Steve said in a tone that was almost a plea.

I craved his arms around me so badly it hurt. "What do you mean?"

"Last night you said you wanted to matter. Destiny, you do matter. More than anything. You are why I do what I do, but I can't do it anymore. It's killing us and, more importantly, it's killing you. I'm not going to work past six anymore. I'm not going to work on Sundays. If the hardware store fails because of it, well then it does."

"What are you talking about?"

"You asked me to support you while you wrote your books. I did. You asked me to support you when you opened your store. I did, and was glad to. But we're running out of money and if I'm going to make what we need, I have to work those hours. You can't handle them, so you'll have to pay your own bills."

My eyes filled and overflowed. Every bit of fight went out of me. "I'm doing the best that I can. And, Steve, I work just as hard as you do. What do want from me?"

"I don't know. Maybe you need to lay off your staff."

I gasped, unwilling to stomach the thought. "I can't do that. She needs this job."

"Well, then maybe *you* need to get a different job."

I stood in the middle of the universe. Its vast expanse spread out cold and empty. If I didn't move, didn't breathe, I might not drift alone into eternity.

Did he not value me at all? What of the work I did for our center, for him, for the goddamned hardware store? Surely he didn't mean what he said. I loved what we had built, our customers, what we did for the world. He must know I couldn't just give it up.

"Steve. Honey, please. Why are you saying this to me?"

He rubbed his face with both hands. The white stubble on his unshaved chin caught the morning light. "Because I've been listening. You don't believe me, but I have. And hearing you. I don't know who I am."

15

When we began this journey, I wore a size sixteen. Now I sported a comfortable size eight. We had shed a person between us—a whopping 120 pounds—and, in the process, lost ourselves.

I could name the age-old battle we waged and justify the positions each of us held, but couldn't find a way off the battlefield. I am a feminist. So is Steve. We support equal rights for women and live our lives with that conviction in mind. Nevertheless, our weight gain and its subsequent loss forced us to confront feminist issues we had previously only faced intellectually.

Steve defined himself as the provider. My financial independence, or lack of it, remained irrelevant in the face of his fundamental identity. He would take care of his family. As I demanded more—respect for my time and efforts and meaningful, non-work-related interaction—he did his best to accommodate, but the stress squeezed him. If he couldn't provide for me, if the way he worked caused me to suffer, who was he?

Battling myself as much as him, I recalled his earlier statement. "You can't have it both ways." I had never been more vulnerable, more afraid. What Steve had thrown out required a choice. Step up or shut up. I had forced us into intractable positions and one of us would break.

He sat across the table. Pain hung on his face like moss on an old, craggy tree and I shivered against the knowledge that he would sacrifice anything for me. Even under this unbearable weight, he held his shoulders straight. The air between us vibrated with the tension of his waiting.

"What do you need from me?" I asked.

He pursed his lips, blew out a breath. "Do you remember telling me that losing your art meant losing your meaning? That without it, you didn't feel like your life had a purpose?"

I nodded, sometimes felt that still. Steve reached out his hand as if to touch me, but didn't. Instead, he laid it limp on the table, fingers trembling on dry teak. "Destiny, the work I do to support us is my meaning."

In my head, the chorus of an old, country song sang. "She keeps the home fires burning..." My heart sank. Would this always be my role? Could I never shake free the shackles of tradition and stand next to him, equal and free?

"You need me to be your base, your haven," I said.

He didn't reply, but his eyes pleaded and I knew what he had done for me. The support and security he'd provided when I needed to stay home and write were as great a sacrifice as what he asked from me now.

Putting my hand over his, I whispered, "I can do that."

His shoulders relaxed, their burden lifted. He stood and held open his arms. I came into them like an ocean meets the shore after a storm, a churning rage of sand, debris, and waves. My tears spilled, and when he kissed me, I tasted their salt. He felt like home, like sun-warmed rocks.

October arrived. The sky deepened into a brilliant blue. One afternoon, Steve made an effort and carved a space for us in the midst of our chaos. We drove to the ski basin and parked near our favorite trail. Aspen leaves littered the ground like gold fairy coins. He walked ahead of me, arms swinging. Already, ice clung to rocks in a clear, tiny creek and the first dusting of snow graced the mountain peaks. I breathed deep, inhaling crisp air laced with pine. The dogs bounded through a meadow, tongues lolling wide. Halfway up the mountain, he pulled off his shirt and stuck it through his belt. His back glistened with sweat. I pulled at the tank top sticking to my chest, looked around and thought, Hell, why not? Sun on skin, a light breeze on breasts—these released my wildness. Steve slowed, took my hand, and grinned.

Oh, God, that smile. Those sparkling eyes. The word love couldn't encompass what I felt for him.

Voices up the trail made me freeze. I struggled to get my shirt back on before people rounded the bend. Steve tossed me his and I pulled it over my head. As they came into view, I felt the sharp bite of restriction, the pinch of unfair rules. What would have happened had I been braver? I doubted the sight of my sagging breasts would have sent those people screaming or incited an uncontrollable lust. At worst, I would have embarrassed them. Once again, the oily tang of shame coated my tongue and the bright day dimmed.

I wanted to be one of those women who dared to eat a peach and disturb the universe. Enraged by the onslaught of laws against women, gang rapes in India, purity balls, and other such events, I railed against rape culture and misogyny at home, yet seldom signed petitions. I didn't go to protests or add my name to feminist lists. Steve encouraged my participation in the online dialog, arguing my voice might have weight, but I feared exposure. I wanted things to change, but refused to be part of that change. That afternoon on the trail, I heard his words again. "You can't have it both ways."

As always, the knowledge called forth a grimace and I wrestled with the issue's complexity. Would I be more equal if I took a job? Did a paycheck justify the financial risk to our businesses? Maybe, I thought. At least then I would be independent. But would it make a difference in our relationship? I couldn't imagine it. When I had been a full time sculptor, his life had dominated our conversations and our fights then often touched on the fact that he seldom remembered to ask about my day. Taking a job would obliterate the intimacy between us. If I did it, our lives would revolve around his work, his businesses, and his needs. And, if he truly needed me to be his meaning, where did that leave me?

Be assertive. Lean in. Speak your mind. Pay your bills. Take a self-defense class or carry a gun, but while you're doing it, be a woman. During times of segregation, separate but equal was an acceptable attitude. In my conversations with Steve, I heard him say different but equal. Was that the same thing?

He liked to tell this joke when talking about the balance of power in relationships:

On their wedding night, a young couple is in a hotel. The woman comes out of the bathroom wearing slinky lingerie. The man puts up his hand and says, "Stop right there." She thinks this is a little strange, but does what he asks. He undoes the buttons on his pants, takes them off, and hurls them at her. In a voice she's never heard, he says, "There. Pick those up. Put them on." She obliges, game for a little role-play, but when she takes her hands away, the pants fall to the floor. "I can't wear those. They're way too big for me," she says. The man snorts. "Yeah. That's right. You just remember that. I wear the pants in this family." The woman smiles sweetly. Slowly, she inches off her panties in a deliberate strip tease and tosses them to her husband. "Okay. Now you put those on," she says. He examines the tiny garment and replies. "I can't get into these." The wife says, "That's right, honey. You just remember that until you change your attitude."

The joke always elicited laughs and the subtle sexism inherent in it went unnoticed by most. What the woman in the joke should have done is packed up her things and left. The balance of power in a relationship shouldn't depend on the man's easy access to sex.

16

The grand opening of the hardware store was a huge success. More than a thousand people turned out and our center thrummed with their excitement. That night, exhausted and proud, Steve toasted me. "This wouldn't have happened without you. This was your marketing."

We clinked glasses and I accepted the compliment, but the marketing was a sore spot. During the buildup to the event, he had shoved it aside as less important and his actions had triggered multiple fights. Now, his belated recognition of my efforts felt false in my heart.

Be the base, I cautioned myself. What's past is past.

I sipped my whiskey appreciatively. We had stopped at the store on our way home and bought the good stuff. "Do you think, now that we're through this, we can plan some real time off?" I asked.

"Absolutely. When?"

I thought about it. "January, after the holiday rush."

"Where do you want to go?"

"It doesn't really matter. I just need to stop."

My body shook with exhaustion and I couldn't remember the last time I'd slept through the night. I hadn't shared with Steve the details of my dreams, how often they occurred, or how strange his body felt. Occasionally, when the vibe in a club made me extra uneasy, I'd make up an excuse to go home, keeping fear to myself so he wouldn't see me as weak. I also hadn't told him of my anxiety attacks. They were unexplainable, and I didn't want him to think me crazy, even though I questioned that myself.

For months while we talked and worked, fought, danced, and laughed, voices once silenced whispered in my head. "You're ugly. You're a coward. You're nothing." Throughout my adult life, every new plateau of success had unleashed their fury. The only way to shut them up was to embark in pursuit of the next. We had gotten the damned hardware store open to huge accolades. On its first anniversary, my store operated in the black. I had written myself a paycheck, tucked it neatly into my wallet, and thanked God that this month, at least, I wouldn't have to ask Steve for money. I had maintained my goal weight in spite of the recent stress, and our marriage, though bruised, remained intact. I should have been basking in glory, but the anxiety attack that hit me as I sipped my whiskey was the worst yet.

Red-eyed snakes slithered through my intestines and curled hideously around liver and kidneys. My heart leapt in my chest like a frog toward a pond, hippety hop, hippety hop. My stomach cramped. Before Steve could see what was happening, I hurried to the bathroom. On the toilet, I kept very still and clenched my teeth. Breathing deep through my nose, I prayed. "Please, God, let it pass." The soundless words were a familiar litany. Sweat broke out on my upper lip and coated my chest. Its stench made me queasy and I clamped down harder to hold the bile back. Then, failing, I dropped to my knees and retched.

Steve poked his head through the door. "Are you okay?" he asked.

I wiped the back of my hand across my mouth. "Cake," I replied.

"Too rich?"

Nodding my head, I fought another battle and lost. Vomit forced its way through my fingers and splattered across the toilet seat. The acid, like poison, burned my eyes as I heaved. When finally I'd voided everything, I rinsed my mouth and brushed my teeth. I made it back to the table on trembling legs and sank into my chair.

Steve looked at me, worried. "Anything I can do for you?"

I nodded, swallowed, and replied, "Whisky, neat." That made him smile, and I was relieved.

"Do you still want to go out?" he asked. "I mean it's fine if you don't. I'd understand."

We had planned to celebrate in town with a sushi dinner and dancing to our favorite band. I wouldn't disappoint him. He had worked too hard for this night and I didn't want to admit the anxiety attacks.

"Absolutely. Let's get dressed," I replied.

Saturday night excitement. Neon lights flashing beer advertisements. Piped music on an outside patio and cold air scented with perfume. Inside, an antique bicycle hung over the bar and chefs in white hats flashed extra sharp knives.

We found a table in the back, put our napkins in our laps, and ordered without glancing at the menu—a large hot sake and a five-piece salmon sashimi each. As I dipped the first succulent bite into its soy sauce bath, the last traces of anxiety vanished. The salmon caressed my tongue, sweet and soft. Across from me, Steve shone.

He swallowed and moaned. "Oh, God. It's so good."

"You were amazing today," I said. "Absolutely amazing." The paper lantern above his head made his honey-colored skin luminescent, even as it hooded his eyes. Exhaustion would set in later, but right now he was exuberant.

"God, I had so much fun! Can you believe how many people showed up?"

"I know. I ordered cake for five hundred and thought it was too much. I think it was gone by noon."

"You know the True Value rep was there for a while? He covers thirty stores and said he hasn't seen an opening like that ever."

I raised my glass to him. "Good job, babe. Good job."

We talked over the day, sharing highlights. His staff had performed exceptionally well in spite of the snafu with the credit card machines. The kids had loved the chocolate hammers. People appreciated the low gondolas and ancient tools decorating the walls.

"How'd you do today?" he asked.

"Best day yet. I did the numbers. I ended the year in the black."

We had timed his grand opening with my anniversary party and the event had exceeded my wildest expectations. "You know the best thing? People aren't even holiday shopping yet."

"You've done an incredible job, Destiny. I've never seen anything like it. No one ends their first year in the black."

I grinned. "Yep, and doubled my inventory too!"

Steve put up his hand and I slapped it. Then he caught my wrist and kissed it. "I love you. More than I can say. More than there are words."

"I know, darlin', and I love you."

Dinner finished, we headed downtown and strolled around the plaza until the music started, hand in hand and still talking. In a doorway, Steve stopped and kissed me hard. My back against cold stucco, the weight of him pressed against my chest—hot breath, lips soft and insistent.

"Get a room!" someone yelled.

I giggled. We heard this comment often—at work, at the airport, on the way to a public restroom—and it baffled me. Sex sells everything from toothpaste to spa treatments. We are barraged with it daily, but while advertising and the film industry make it fantasy, people shame the reality. What would it take to normalize our culture's twisted views on sexuality?

"And when we get behind closed doors and she lets her hair hang down..." I sang Charlie Rich's song badly, softly, into Steve's ear.

He grabbed my head, turned me slightly, and kissed me again. "God, I love you!" he said.

The bar smelled of greasy food, stale beer, and floor wax. We took our usual table and Steve held up two fingers to our regular waitress. The band began to play. The room filled. The dance floor stayed empty. Steve looked at me, jerked his head toward the stage. "Are you ready?"

We were almost always the first to dance and it still made me a little uneasy. I closed my eyes, shutting out the crowd, and stepped close to him. Steve shielded me with his arms, putting a bubble around me until I relaxed enough to feel safe. Then we moved in earnest, thigh to thigh, and hips grinding. The song ended with us laughing from the sheer joy of it. We made our way back to the table and downed half of our drinks. Songs came one after another: a little rock, a little blues, the occasional country-western twang. Other people began to dance and I momentarily resented the loss of room, the bodies restricting my movements, the smell of rank sweat and cheap perfume. Then Steve's eyes and quick grin put me in my groove again.

Breathing hard, I signaled for a break and maneuvered my way off the floor.

Steve caught up with me and grabbed my arm. "See that guy at the bar, the one in the cap?" he asked.

I scanned the row of people: a few couples and a lot of single men. "The skinny one toward the end?" I asked.

"Yeah. He can't take his eyes off you and I don't blame him a bit. You are moving so well tonight, my sexy, sexy wife."

I smiled, pleased by the compliment, and tamped down my threat assessment. Nothing would happen here, not while I was with him.

We danced until our legs gave out. Steve went to pay the tab and hit the bathroom. I waited for him at the end of the bar closest to the exit, where cold air blew mercifully on my hot, damp skin. The club had been around a long time and shelves piled high with ancient memorabilia lined the room. I put my elbows on the bar and cradled my chin, trying to guess what had motivated the collection. A miniature fire truck from the forties sat next to a snow globe. An enameled, plaster bear leaned against a bongo drum. A crowd of people jostled around me, moving in and out the open door.

Suddenly, an arm pressed against my back and pinned me to the bar. A hand lifted my dress and crawled between my thighs, fingers wriggling. Time stopped. My breath froze. I couldn't move or find sound to protest. He probed me once and then was gone. The world began to spin again.

17

I didn't tell Steve. I didn't tell anyone. What would I say, and to what end? The thing had happened, but no real damage was done. Some creep copped a feel. That was it, or so I told myself then.

When Steve returned from the bathroom, I managed a wan smile.

"Are you okay? You look a little pale," he said.

"Fine, just a bit of the spins."

"I didn't think you drank that much."

"I don't know. I guess maybe I did."

At home, Steve made love to me. I hurled myself against him, willing his body to make me clean, to eradicate any trace of fingers wriggling. I turned rage to violence and shame to lust in a dance that couldn't be passionate enough.

When he fell asleep, I disentangled our limbs and lay rigid on my side of the bed. Maybe I'd willed this. Maybe my fear created the reality. Why hadn't I been more alert? How could I have been so trusting? What the hell did I project that made men think they could touch me without consent?

In the movies, glass doesn't break in an instant. A tiny impact makes a hairline crack. Seconds later, a truck rumbles by. That innocuous tremor shatters the glass. My shattering didn't happen that fast. In retrospect, I wish it had.

I had survived rape at nineteen. In comparison, this was nothing, but it brought the memories back. My nightmares became a waking reality as I relived that previous experience again and again. Then, too, I hadn't fought back. No police report recorded the incident. No charges were brought. I believed with every fiber of my being that resisting the attack would have incited greater violence, perhaps even my death. While I knew the man's name, where he lived, and that he would likely do it again, I didn't do anything to him because, in spite of my bruises, the likelihood of conviction was slim. The shame of inaction fed the voices in my head. I blamed myself for both events and tore myself to shreds, even though I knew it was ridiculous.

Just after Thanksgiving, Steve came up behind me when I didn't have my hearing aids in place. He put his hand on my shoulder and I jumped so hard I screamed.

"Oh, God. Honey, I'm sorry," he said, but his mouth twitched.

"It's not fucking funny. Jesus, Steve, what were you thinking?"

He tensed. "I'm sorry. I didn't mean anything."

When he stiffened, I went cold. A shiver shook me. I couldn't take his hard edges, compressed lips, and bristling masculinity. The dam inside me broke. "I can't. I just can't..."

"Destiny, what's wrong?"

At first, the words got stuck in my sobs. Finally, gulping air, I told him about the man at the bar. Afternoon sunlight slanted across the table, highlighting the wood grains. The dogs whined at the door and Steve got up to let them in. He poured two whiskies and handed me one. I slammed it, hard. He tipped the bottle again and refilled my glass.

Thoughts flickered across his face like cloud shadows on the mountains. I couldn't read them. At first, he simply held me. The air went out of him at my story, and he pulled me so close it hurt. Then he sunk his chin on the top of my head and whispered, "Oh, Destiny. I am so sorry."

Now, sitting across from me, he silently nursed his drink.

"Say something, Steve. Please."

Muscles jumped in his jaw. "You never saw who it was?"

I shook my head, embarrassed. "No."

He contemplated this for a minute. Then, slowly, he said, "What I don't understand is why you didn't scream. Why, once he'd released you, you didn't turn around?"

He doesn't believe me, I thought. My heart sank, taking the last of my strength with it. "I couldn't. I was too shocked. I froze like a deer in the headlights. Steve, I'm sorry." I felt soiled, used, and less than he deserved.

"You're never a deer in the headlights."

"Well, I was this time. What do you want from me? Why are we even talking about this?"

Steve searched my face. "I'm just trying to understand. You could have stopped him. We could have called the police."

Something in me snapped. "I would never have called the police. What would I say, huh? Oh, this guy randomly fingered me with fifty people present and nobody saw a damned thing. Oh, and yes my dress was short, and yes, I'd been dirty dancing. Oh, and one more thing, I'd been drinking. We could go to the hospital and they could scrape my vagina for his DNA, and then they'd tell me I probably liked it because I didn't even fucking scream!"

Steve sagged in his chair as if all the bones in his body had suddenly melted. His jaw went slack and his eyes glittered, though the tears didn't spill.

My breath came ragged and fast. I stood and went to the window. A cold wind howled around the house. Dead leaves pin-wheeled across the flagstone walkway. From the branches of a juniper tree, a crow took flight. It cawed once, flapped dull black wings, and soared into the gathering clouds. I crossed my arms over my chest, shivering.

Steve came up behind me and put his hands on my shoulders. "Don't be sorry," he said.

"What?"

"Don't be sorry. You don't have to apologize to me or anyone else."

I turned to him and buried my face in his chest. "Oh God, Steve. I'm so ashamed."

"Destiny. Listen to me. It's not your fault. You did nothing wrong. I just wish you'd told me. That's all."

"It is my fault. I didn't fight, when I was a kid or now. I didn't call for help. I just let those bastards take what they wanted." I moved away from him and poured another drink with trembling hands. "Don't you see, Steve? I'm nothing. I'm just a piece of meat. I was in that bar and I was in that bed, and you can't say anything to change that."

Night came. A thin moon hovered on the horizon, briefly visible as clouds whipped past. Emotion etched deep lines in Steve's face. He had failed to protect me, failed to avenge me, and now I wouldn't be comforted or reassured. I just wanted to be numb, or at least drunk.

"There is nothing you could have done," Steve said again.

"You keep saying that, but I don't know that and neither do you."

"I do know it. It's physics. It doesn't matter how strong you are or how many techniques you have. If somebody that much bigger than you gets a hold on you, you're not getting up."

He kept pushing, needing to do something to make it better, make it right, until I felt backed in a corner and trapped by his words.

"Prove it," I whispered.

"What?"

"*Prove it!*"

"What are you talking about?"

"Do it, Steve. Hold me down and *prove* it to me."

His eyes narrowed. "Are you sure you want that?"

I nodded. I wanted to fight as hard as I could and fail, needed that knowledge in my bones.

I rose from the table and staggered toward the bedroom. He followed. As I opened the door, he grabbed me, pinning my arms to my sides and hoisting me off the floor. In seconds, he threw me on the bed, trapped my hands in his, and rendered me powerless. I kicked, wriggled, and bucked to no avail. He spread my thighs with his knee and pressed himself against me.

"I could take you right now and there is nothing you could do to stop me," Steve said hoarsely.

"No! Don't! Stop!"

And then, suddenly, it wasn't my beloved husband on top of me. It was him, the man who'd raped me so long ago. I smelled cocaine, cologne, and stale beer breath, heard the grunts coming out of his mouth. His hard cock ground against my jeans, bruising my pelvis. I felt my wrists would snap. Terror clawed my belly, turned my veins to ice. I saw red briefly, then my world went black.

18

I woke naked in my car, a flashlight in my face. After that, I remember little: a sheriff at our dining room table, the bite of handcuffs on my wrists. In the hospital, someone tugged at my shirt and I went crazy. There was a period of time when I curled fetus-like on a floor crying, "Please don't hurt me again." At one point, several people grabbed my arms and legs and carried me somewhere. At another, a sheriff pushing me through a door jerked my cuffed wrists up, tearing my skin and wrenching my shoulder. Eventually, I woke again, shivering on the floor of a jail cell.

God it was cold. I couldn't stop shaking. Pain coursed like fire down my arm and I couldn't move it at all. I wore my own clothes, but had no shoes. One of my socks had a hole. The tiny cell lacked bed or toilet, its only furnishing a torn and dirty moving blanket. Someone watched me through a window in the heavy steel door.

"I want a phone call and a doctor. I think my arm is broken," I yelled.

The person didn't reply.

"What am I doing here? Why? He raped me. Don't you understand? *He* raped *me*."

Silence met my questions. Then a loud clang startled me and I screamed.

I lay on that floor for hours, begging for medical attention and a phone call. When a woman brought a breakfast tray, I demanded them again, reiterating that I had been raped. She told me I should have had a rape kit done at the hospital, but I'd been a bad girl so I didn't get one. I could make no sense of her words or what had happened. I only knew my terror had turned to rage.

At seven in the morning, they took me to see a psychiatrist. By then, bits and pieces of the previous night had come back and I had a growing sense that my marriage was dead. The man interviewed me to ensure I wouldn't kill myself, which baffled me completely. Then, out of compassion or because I wore him down, he broke the rules and let me call Steve.

My hands shook as I punched the number. What would he say? I'd hurt him. I knew that, but how? He answered on the first ring. His voice, eager and scared, gave me hope.

It took eleven hours to see a medical doctor. To my horror, I knew him. He put my shoulder back in its socket and suggested I sue. He also sent me to the hospital for an x-ray to ensure more serious damage hadn't been done. The guards took me in chains. Wearing a thin, red shirt that marked me as a prisoner, I shuffled in open-toed slippers through snow and mud, teeth chattering against the cold. Because of the handcuffs, I couldn't cover my face and shame chilled my bones.

I returned to the jail in a sling. This time, the guards put me in a cell with a bed. I lay on it willing myself not to panic. The walls felt so close. I couldn't see anything out the slit in the door. Fluorescent lights buzzed. The roomed reeked of urine and fear-tainted sweat. A high, narrow window let in a sliver of light, but was angled to obscure the sky. I stared up at it and prayed, "Please, God, don't let him leave me."

The guards came again early in the evening. When the door opened, relief made my knees weak. In a small, white room off a large corridor, they handed me a piece of paper, gave me back my shoes and coat, and told me to wait. Then they left, locking the door behind them, and subsequently forgot me. Minutes ticked by. I heard voices come and go. I waited an eternity before I banged on the door.

Release wasn't sweet. They turned me out into a parking lot. Halogen lights lit the falling snow. The sling I wore prevented me from zipping my coat. Worse, I had no idea how to get home. I paced, trying to stay warm. A cruiser pulled up and I asked the sheriff to borrow a phone. He said no.

Tears froze to my face as I huddled against the building where a shaft of light shone through a set of locked glass doors. Desperate, I pushed the intercom button and begged the person on the other end to allow me a phone call. She denied me again and again. Eventually, someone took pity, told the woman to let me in and give me a phone. This time when Steve answered, his voice was cold.

I read the sheriff's report while I waited for a ride. I had apparently scratched Steve's arm and twisted his balls. Later, when a friend of his dropped me at the hardware store, Steve told me I had gone insane. He had climbed off me when I told him to stop, but then I went after him like a wild thing released from a cage. We struggled. He managed to get away. I howled at the moon while he hid in our camper and called 911.

I cried during his telling, cried harder when he took me stiffly in his arms. Doing so, he broke a court order. Our marriage, or what was left of it, was no longer our own.

I had heard of flashbacks, of course, but never dreamed I would experience one. Over the next few weeks, I barely functioned. Steve didn't trust me and I didn't trust myself. A loud noise, the sight of a cop on the side of the road, the unexpected voice of someone I didn't know hurled me out of reality.

At work, I told people I'd dislocated my shoulder in a fall. I hated the lie, but couldn't speak the truth. At home, I wept at the deep gouges in Steve's arm. Even after he'd forgiven me, my injured shoulder prohibited our cuddling. The irony of the situation strangled me. I had been victimized twice. Because of it I went to jail where, once again, a man assaulted me.

As my court date approached, my anxiety deepened. I vomited when we tried to make love and stopped sleeping completely. Rather than face my nightmares, I listened to an audio book and occasionally dozed on the couch. The arrest, and what preceded it, haunted me day and night, but I couldn't take time off in the middle of my holiday season. There was no respite.

Steve suffered too. That was the worst part. Looking at his gaunt face, hearing the hollow in his laugh, I wanted to die. I caused his misery. I broke our marriage. I had lost my mind. There was no going back to what we had, to who we were before that awful night. Though we stopped dancing, paying attention to what we ate, and every behavior that might trigger another incident, we would never be the same.

The court made my release conditional. Technically, Steve and I weren't supposed to be in the same house, much less the same bed. Touch was prohibited, along with alcohol and drugs. While we ignored everything but the last, the order hovered over us like a dagger. So did the question of my sanity, yet somewhere deep inside me a small voice whispered a startling truth. "You fought back," it said. And so I had.

19

L ike a flame in the dark, that small voice guided me. Sometimes it flickered. Once it almost went out, but then the wind inside me quieted and I found it again. I had shattered because there is only so much bottled grief and walled rage a body can take. A storm had ripped through me, and now, walking through the destruction it wreaked, that voice said, "No more. You've had enough."

At my first court appearance, over-dressed and shaking, Steve and I held hands covertly. He had spoken with the district attorney and would not be a witness for the prosecution, but the charges remained and the court would have its say.

Painted in tans and browns, the blandness of the courtroom rendered the crowd of defendants clownish. Tattoos, glittering shoes, too tight shirts, and stringy hair decorated bodies thin, thick, and in despair. I did not belong there. When the clerk called my name, I didn't think my legs would hold as I made my way to the podium. The judge read the charges against me and I fought to control my tears. When asked how I pleaded, I was surprised to find a working voice.

"Not guilty," I said. The lie choked my throat. I had hurt the man I loved in more ways than one.

Steve took me for coffee after the judge accepted my plea, and I couldn't meet his eyes. Instead, I shredded a paper napkin and left my muffin untouched. The restaurant clattered and clanged. Someone dropped a fork. Another stacked dirty plates. A cappuccino machine screamed.

Steve grabbed my hand. "Destiny, look at me. We're going to get through this."

I nodded. "I'm sorry, Steve. I love you and I am so very sorry."

"I know you are. And I understand. It all makes sense now."

"What does?"

"Our fights. Your nightmares. I didn't know what was happening. Now I do."

My eyes filled. Though we had stabilized and our fights had abated, my anxiety hadn't. How would we get through this if I remained a ticking bomb?

I looked at Steve then, plagued by a nagging thought. "Can I ask you a hard question?"

"Sure. What?" he said.

"Why did you call the cops?"

He paled. "Honey, you don't remember most of that night. I was afraid. For both of us. I didn't know what else to do."

"You could have stopped it."

Steve shook his head. "No. I mean, sure. I could have held you down, but what good would that do? You were in flashback, right? Reliving a rape? What would getting violent and using my strength have done?"

"Made it worse, I guess."

"Exactly. I did it to keep us both safe."

"Okay. I agree. It was the right thing to do. I just had to make sure you weren't punishing me."

"Destiny, I love you. More than I can say. I wouldn't do that." He squeezed my hand. "I was proud of you today."

"For what?"

"Your courage in the courtroom."

No, I thought. That wasn't courage. My actions in the courtroom had been of necessity, but I knew what courage was.

Later, at work, I took a deep breath and Googled my symptoms. Anxiety. Nightmares. Flashback. PTSD was for warriors, not people like me.

I researched frantically, but the deeper I dug, the more convinced I became. I needed help. If I didn't get it, me and my marriage were done.

That first step fed my tiny flame. The knowledge I gleaned proved my sanity. The changes in my life over the last year had built pressure greater than I could bear. A dormant volcano had erupted. Now the lava had to cool. I picked up the phone, called the rape crisis center, and made an appointment for evaluation. If they accepted me as a patient, I would do the work necessary to heal my wounds.

On the drive to the crisis center, my slick palms slipped on the steering wheel. Somehow, I managed to park. Shame crawled like a swarm of ants through my arms, legs, and belly and I found it hard to breathe. In spite of the frigid air, I sweated profusely on the walk to the clinic door. Inside, I kept my eyes to the floor. Every single person I passed knew without question that I had been raped. Worse, they knew I couldn't handle it on my own. My presence there confirmed it as if I'd stood on a stage and waved a flag. The receptionist offered me tea. I accepted gratefully and clung to the steaming mug like it would save me. Green plants, a white stone sculpture, blue rugs, and comfortable armchairs decorated a pleasant lobby. Magazines graced a glass coffee table, but reading was beyond my capabilities. I waited.

The interview was brief. The therapist explained the treatment. If her team accepted me, she thought six sessions would be enough.

"Just six? Really?" I asked.

"We do a different kind of therapy for PTSD. It's called Brainspotting and it doesn't require you to dredge up your past or talk through your emotions. It's fast and has been proven very effective in these kinds of cases."

My worry dimmed. I had dreaded the probability of having to discuss the details of my life, all the traumatic events. "When do you make a decision?"

The therapist looked at me, her face a mask of sympathy. "We'll meet this week. We'll call you as soon as we know," she said.

I nodded and stood to go.

I began my sessions in January. They assigned me a different therapist. Melissa was younger than me by more than a decade. Seeing her for the first time, I figured I didn't have a prayer for recovery. She was slim and graceful, but the scarf she wore around her neck looked part of a costume, as if she too was hiding something. We spent the first half hour filling out paperwork and documenting my commitment. When Melissa asked me why I was there, I thought for a minute. My answer surprised us both. "I'm here because I love someone more than the pain." With those words, my walls began crumbling.

The therapy taught me breathing techniques. Melissa led me through guided mediation and gave me homework each week. Identify triggers. Pay attention to how I react. Make notes on my response to different situations. After the first two sessions, my anxiety lessened. I was not only learning to breathe, I was learning to speak.

When Steve and I took a vacation in January, I brought my homework with me. We talked at length about my therapy, how it felt to be a woman in the world, and the subtleties of sexual discrimination, but mostly we played. This in itself was new for me. I had always hated crowds and condescended to those who engaged in silly, adult games. My idea of a good vacation was to find a quiet corner and read. This time, however, something in me was different. On the cruise ship, we danced for hours every day at the pool, in the halls and bars. At night, we went to shows, participated in the games, and then danced again until trembling legs sent us back to our cabin.

Oh, how we laughed. I gasped for breath watching Steve perform as one of the Village People. My sides ached and tears streamed down my cheeks when he sang YMCA with the other men. If the dance floor wasn't crowded, we pulled people to their feet and got the party going again. In between these events, I practiced my lessons. No negative self talk. Watch the emotion roll in and then decide what to do with it. Don't fight it, but don't let it rule you. It's just a feeling.

In Belize, we left the crowds and tourist activities to explore by ourselves. We wandered away from the port and down side streets until we found a cemetery filled with ancient graves. Gray stone etched with black, a luscious lawn of bright green grass. This one died from illness. That one was killed in a shipwreck. Though the stones were eroded and hard to read, all the souls had been beloved and commended to God. Humidity and heat drove us to a local bar that was little more than a shack. It perched above the harbor on stilts. A thatched roof and plank walls did nothing to keep the birds out. We sucked down the first cold beer and ordered another. Our casual conversation was continually interrupted by a waiter who let us know he could procure anything we needed from weed to hookers. In the distance, multi-story granite buildings framed downtown.

"I wonder how long they've been there," Steve said.

"Seventeen hundreds, maybe. Maybe longer," I replied.

"I wonder what this place looks like after a hurricane. I mean, those buildings are gonna survive, but what about these?" He gestured to the shack.

I nodded. "That's what I feel like, you know."

"What do you mean?" he asked.

"Like I was this shack. A hurricane hit and now it's bright because the buildings are gone and the land is littered with broken pieces. I can see all the pieces of me. The problem is, I don't know yet which of them to keep."

Steve kissed me and stood. "Dance with me, my love." He extended a hand.

I took it and we danced as if alone in the bar, close in each other's arms.

20

Eventually, the state dismissed the domestic violence charges against me. The therapy sessions taught me a lot, but more importantly, they released the worst of what I had carried since my rape at nineteen. Slowly, almost imperceptibly, I changed.

My dreams became moments of triumph instead of horror. In them, I subdued my attackers, built a new house with a room in it just for me, and in one particularly powerful instance, gave birth to a daughter I knew as my true self.

Together, Steve and I redefined normal. He had gained fifteen pounds over the winter and while I had maintained my weight, we refocused on health and shared experience. We resumed dancing, though not as often, and went back to eating well. Steve lost the weight. I stopped hating myself.

At first, I made a conscious effort. I vowed to never again compare my body to that of another woman and determined to find beauty in every woman I met. When a negative thought surfaced, I reframed it and told the truth. Messy hair has nothing to do with beauty. Stretch marks are an important part of life.

In late February, I attended a trade show in Las Vegas. After one of my suppliers introduced new features making their handbags more competitive, I asked a question the saleswoman couldn't answer. She called a man over and Steve put out a hand. Instantly, the saleswoman and I ceased to exist. The man launched into a full product description and would only look and talk to Steve, who rolled his eyes at me. The saleswoman blanched, but the man failed to notice. I began to steam, but instead of interrupting the man, I pulled the saleswoman away.

"Who is that guy?" I asked.

"He's the founder and CEO."

Shaking my head in disgust, I said, "I have to tell you, if we hadn't already done business and I didn't have confidence in your products, you would have just lost a customer."

The woman rattled off what seemed a well practiced defense. "Oh. He's not usually like that. He's great to work for and our staff is almost all women."

Listening, it occurred to me that this was a perfect example of what women do to themselves. "Why am I telling you this? I should be talking to him."

Her mouth opened and she put out a hand as if to stop me, but I ignored her. As I approached Steve, he glanced at me, grinned, and mouthed, "Uh oh."

I touched the man's arm, stopping him mid-sentence. "Excuse me. Can I talk to you for a minute?" I asked.

The CEO knew what I was about. Steve had already said something, but it hadn't made a difference. "Sorry about that, it's just that Steve introduced himself and—"

"And you made an assumption that was incredibly rude. This is my business. I am the decision maker. I told your saleswoman this, but decided you needed to hear it too. If I didn't know your product, I wouldn't do business with you."

He started to make excuses.

I refused them.

Eventually, he listened. Our subsequent dialog benefited us both.

Over the next several weeks, I met men's eyes at the bars and forced them to look at more than my body. Sometimes, they blushed. More often, they smiled. Without thinking about it, the word "sorry" retreated from my vocabulary. When a man condescended to me, I responded directly instead of fuming in silence.

One night at our favorite club, Steve and I owned the dance floor. My body felt fluid. He moved with exquisite grace. We danced shamelessly. A few people sat at the bar, fewer at the tables, and we had room to let loose. Once again, the world dissolved and I abandoned myself to the man I loved.

We knew the band well. Trying to improve their act, they practiced a vague comedy routine in between songs. At one point, we returned to our table to catch our breath and sip our drinks. A guitarist took the mic and made a few innocuous comments. Failing to evoke laughter from the crowd, he pointed at a woman at the bar and said, "She needs to dance." Then he pointed at me and said, "And she needs to get a room."

For the first time in my life, I didn't take it personally. I leaned back in my chair, threw him a finger, and grinned. He bowed, gesturing a fake apology, and the music resumed. Later, when the band took a break, I approached the stage. The guitarist glanced at me warily. I sat down on the scuffed carpet and invited him to join me.

"That was out of line," I said.

"Oh. Sorry. Bad judgment," he replied.

"I don't know if you realize this, but you made me a sexual object in a room full of drunk men. You didn't say we need to get a room. You said I did. My husband was dancing just like me and, honestly, if you'd referred to us both, I would have just thought you a jerk. But you didn't. You made it about me, about my body. You singled me out and tried to shame me. Do you know how hard it is for a woman to be herself in a room like this? You just made it harder for every woman here and I wanted you to know."

He looked at me, mouth agape, then took my hands in his. "I can't tell you how sorry I am and how much I appreciate you telling me. I didn't realize how bad my jokes were and I'm betting I've offended lots more women than you."

I met his gaze. A close cropped beard shone white against his chocolate colored skin. Deep brown eyes reflected his dismay. I smiled. "We're good. Thanks for listening. We'll dance to you again. Hell, you guys are one of our favorite bands."

I made my way back to our table, grinning.

Steve raised his eyebrows. "How was that?" he asked.

"Great. Just great. I wasn't angry or shrill, and he listened. I'd bet money he won't do that again."

"I don't know. He's a man. We don't learn that fast."

"I don't care. I said something and that's a huge step. I'm kinda proud of myself."

Steve smiled, his mouth warm and generous. "I'm proud of you, too, sweetheart. Ready to dance?"

The next morning, I had a Facebook message. The guitarist had found me. This is what the message said: "It is not often you get a hard lesson and recover in this bar band biz. Usually, they just don't come out to see you anymore and you don't have a clue. Hope I have learned my lesson and get to see you again as a fan. I woke with this still on my mind. I wonder if I have caused others to feel off due to my less than sensitive banter? Again, apologies."

I dashed out of my store and found Steve working on a machine. "Look, look. He found me on Facebook and messaged me," I said, waving my phone in his face.

"Who?" Steve asked.

"The guy from last night. It worked, Steve. It worked. Can you believe it?" I read him the note, grinning with glee.

"Wow. I'm impressed," he said. Then he kissed me and added, "Good job."

I left his office and returned to my store. A customer came in and I helped her find a blouse. We laughed and joked until she made a derisive comment about her boobs. I stopped her. "We only have two rules here. One: If you're picking at something because it's uncomfortable, you can't take it home. And two: while you're here, you're beautiful."

She pursed her lips and shook her head. Then she gave me a hug. I smiled to myself, feeling strong.

Epilogue

teve and I had no idea what we would face as we embarked on our plan to lose weight. We thought we were simply dealing with health issues. Instead, we discovered layer upon layer of old wounds, ingrained habits and patterns, and miscommunication.

The steps we took to become physically healthy required us to become mentally and emotionally healthy as well. Steve thought he was a die-hard feminist and the perfect example of what that means in a man. It never occurred to him that misogyny was rooted as deeply in him as it is in our culture at large. The journey required him to learn new methods of communication, but, more importantly, it mandated he embrace new patterns of thinking and discover empathy for experiences he would never have.

Before we began this journey, I thought I had put my rape behind me. Instead, the process revealed shame, guilt, and inadequacy issues long buried or ignored. Our culture needs to change, but as Steve reminded me in so many ways, I had abdicated my responsibility in being part of that change. For what it's worth, I'm adding my voice to the chorus these days.

Steve and I both realize that journeys seldom end. We arrive at a destination just to begin again. The trials we endured through this process strengthened and deepened our love. We got healthy. We learned a great deal about each other and ourselves. Still, we're not done. This is not a stopping place. In fact, we've only just begun.

One of my early readers asked me to write advice here as if I were writing to my newborn daughter. Well, here it is:

My darling, beautiful girl, know that strength is in softness and delight in the world. Do not don armor unless you are at war. Instead, show the world how beautiful you are. Know also that beauty seldom lies in the trappings of your body. It resides in your soul. It shines through your eyes and touch, your compassion, and mind. Grow your mind. Sharpen it. Seek wisdom over knowledge, lead with questions rather than conviction. Most of all, my darling girl, be true to yourself and know that you cannot control all circumstances. Nor should you try. Be fearless. Bad things happen to everyone, but they don't have to end the world.

Thank you for reading! I hope you enjoyed *The Romance Diet* and that you consider leaving a review. Visit me at www.destinyallisonbooks.com and sign up for my newsletter.

Acknowledgements

The Romance Diet would not have been possible without help from my editors, Debra L Hartmann and James Smith, and some very dear friends. I am so grateful to Margaret Bralds, Ana Gonzales Lewis, Nancy Reyner, Andre Gensburger, Diane Thomas, Ted Orland, Nicky Tixier, and Kate Wheeler for their invaluable feedback and support. Thanks also to Kathleen Fallon and Elaine Casquanelli for their honesty, encouragement, and vital contributions to this project. With their help, it is my hope that *The Romance Diet* helps individuals and couples through their own journeys to health and deeper love.

In addition, my deepest gratitude goes to Solace Crisis Treatment Center for their skill, compassion, and expertise. Without this organization, it's questionable whether I would be here at all.

I would be remiss to ignore the women who shop at my store and share their stories, laughter, and tears. Ladies, you inspired me and gave me the courage to write this book. More, you did it by simply being who you are. Thank you so much.

Finally, Steve, thanks for sticking with me through the hardest stuff either of us has known. You are my closest friend, my strongest ally, my deepest love.

Readers Guide

The following quotes from the book and related questions were prepared by Elaine Casquarelli, LMHC and Kathleen (Kitty) Fallon, Ph.D., LMHC, NCC, BCC. Elaine and Kitty have over thirty years of counseling and teaching between them.

The questions they ask can be used with family, friends, and partners to spark introspection, stimulate dialog, and help people take care of themselves and the people they love.

A more comprehensive workbook for those interested in furthering their own growth is in the works. Visit www.destinyallisonbooks.com and sign up for the newsletter to get information on its release.

"I've never been a big breakfast person, but it was Steve's favorite meal. He woke hours before me and loved to have it cooking when I staggered into the kitchen, eyes squinting against the onslaught of daylight. This morning, the sight of all that food repulsed me. I wasn't hungry yet, but not wanting to disappoint him, I broke the yolks and choked down a bite. The smell turned my stomach. Overnight, food had become the enemy."

What is your relationship with food? Other than physical sustenance, what purposes does food serve in your life or relationships?

Has there been a time in your life when you either gained or lost weight to avoid conflict in a relationship or to avoid the attractions of others? If so, describe that experience.

Have a discussion around portion size, food types, and sugar intake. What differences have you noticed in your diet and your health over the years?

What would it mean for you to stop hiding from your body symptoms?

"Identity is a difficult thing. Mine had been deeply tied to financial independence, physical strength, and accolades. Now, without an income of my own and unable to trust my body, my insecurities reared. Was I still sexy? Did Steve resent my lack of a paycheck? Did he see me the way I saw myself—fat, weak, and useless?"

How would you describe your identity, the person you truly are? What do you believe defines you? What do you believe "makes you somebody"?

What would lead you to feel as if you've lost your identity? How connected do you feel to your identity now? Describe any moments when you may feel as if you've lost part of yourself.

How can you maintain your identity when you experience feeling invisible or inconsequential?

"Him, me, us—it was all such a tangled mess. I often wondered what it would be like to be Steve. I could call him self-absorbed, but was he any less so than me? Confidence was the real difference between us. If he angered me, he didn't worry about terrible outcomes. He never walked quickly through a dark parking lot. I imagined living in a world where I could appreciate a stranger's admiring glance without automatically gauging his level of threat. There were so many subtle variations in our day to day experience."

In your experiences, what are men's and women's experiences with success, body image, and self-perception? Explore the similarities and differences.

Discuss your experiences and beliefs around "unfair rules" for men and women.

To what extent do cultural messages about gender expectations shape your relationships?

When have you felt objectified or invisible, not seen in your own right? How did you respond to that experience? How could you support seeing yourself fully in your own right? What recommendations do you have for creating greater visibility for women in our culture/society?

Can you think of a time in your life when you defied traditional gender expectations and experiences? Describe that experience. What was it like? Did it change the way you thought of, felt about, or related to yourself? How did it impact your relationships?

"Something in me snapped. 'I would never have called the police. What would I say, huh? Oh, this guy randomly fingered me with fifty people present and nobody saw a damned thing. Oh, and yes my dress was short, and yes, I'd been dirty dancing. Oh, and one more thing, I'd been drinking. We could go to the hospital and they could scrape my vagina for his DNA, and then they'd tell me I probably liked it because I didn't even fucking scream!'"

Dialog with one another about your experience with trauma.

If you experienced trauma, how have you responded when past trauma emerged again in your life?

What do you need to best support your relationship's health and your individual healing?

"For me, it was different. Though tough as nails on the outside, inside I quivered like the egg on his fork that morning. The artist in me waited always for the next rejection while the woman in me understood her role all too well. Make your man happy. Keep a clean house. Be graceful, demur, and charming. I failed at most of these things, often grotesquely, and my lack reinforced a constant self-doubt. I wanted what Steve had."

What self-doubts and self-critical messages occupy your mind and heart?

How vulnerable and self-critical is your relationship with your body?

Describe times when you diminished who you were for the sake of someone else.

To what extent or under what circumstances are you willing to continue to do so? To what extent are you unwilling to diminish who you are?

How aware are you of your partner's self-doubts and self-critical messages?

What emotions or experiences are you feeling deeply but hiding from others? Does hiding them serve you in any way?

Was there a time in your life when you were afraid to tell the truth about what you wanted or needed? What did you—or do you—need in order to feel safe enough to tell the truth?

How have you tried to keep unwelcome emotions at bay? How have you tried to hide them from your loved ones? Is there someone you can trust to talk to about them? How can we create supportive environments for each other?

"At first, I made a conscious effort. I vowed to never again compare my body to that of another woman and determined to find beauty in every woman I met. When a negative thought surfaced, I reframed it and told the truth. Messy hair has nothing to do with beauty. Stretch marks are an important part of life."

What are the top 10 characteristics you love about your body?

What are the top 10 characteristics you love about other elements of your being?

How can you continue to grow more compassion and love for the physical and non-physical parts of yourself? How can we do this as a society?

In what ways are you noticing your true self inspiring, healing, challenging, loving, and making a difference in our world?

Consider forming an ongoing group to mutually support one another in continuing to glean the wisdom from this book and making healing changes in your lives!

CPSIA information can be obtained
at www.ICGtesting.com
Printed in the USA
FSOW01n0537231215
14580FS